# dévoré

## For Weavers & Knitters

T TS
TRAFALGAR SQUARE
North Pomfret, Vermont

Anne Field

This book is produced using paper that is made from wood grown in managed, sustainable forests. It is natural, renewable and recyclable. The logging and manufacturing processes conform to the environmental regulations of the country of origin.

CIP Catalogue records for this book are available from the British Library and the U.S. Library of Congress.

First published in the United States of America in 2010 by
Trafalgar Square Books
North Pomfret, Vermont 05053

ISBN: 978-157076-460-8

Library of Congress Control Number: 2009937585

Cover design and layout by Bob Anderson for Willson Scott Publishing, Christchurch, New Zealand.

Printed in Taiwan by Sunny Young Printing Company.

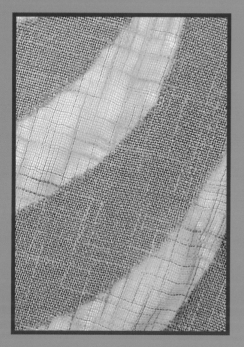

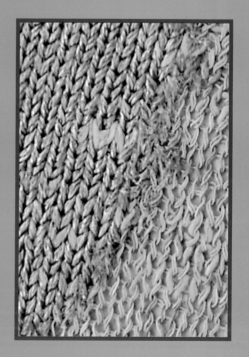

# dévoré

## For Weavers & Knitters

Anne Field

# CONTENTS

Background. What causes dévoré? Safety precautions. Where to get the solution. Kits. Fibres that will burn out. Fibres that will not burn out. Testing fibres. Testing mixed yarns. Yarn size. Wraps per 2.5cm (1in). Tex. Knitted and woven samples.

Yarn mixes. Blended yarns. Mixed yarns. Mixing the yarns yourself. Doubling stand. Spinning yarns together. Shuttles for weaving. Twist amount. Weaving the cloth. Hand-knitting the cloth. Machine-knitting the cloth. Weavettes.

What you need: The process.

Weaving: Random-dyed burn out warp. Random-dyed burn out warp and weft. Random-dyed non-burn out warp. Space-dyed non-burn out warp and weft. Random-dyed non-burn out warp and burn out weft. Random-dyed non-burn out warp and weft. Dyeing complete article after weaving. Dyeing the burn out areas only. Random-dyed burn out weft. Commercially dyed weft yarn. Random-dyed non-burn out weft. Knitting: Random-dyed burn out yarn. Multi-directional scarf. Dyeing the non-burn out yarn. Knitting with a commercially dyed non-burn out yarn (Opal). Dyeing the non-burn out yarn after knitting.

Manufactured dévoré fabric

# ACKNOWLEDGEMENTS

I would like to thank all the people who have helped with this book. Knitters: Margaret Wilson, Kathy McLauchlan, Billee Mutton, Beverley Francis, Lynne Nicholls. Machine knitter: Heather Phillips. Embroiderer: Barbara Johns. Weavers: Alison Francis, Janie Gummer, Amy Norris, John Mullarkey, and felter Anne Willitts. My Fibre Forum workshop at Orange in 2008 gave me added information and tested my publisher's patience as I added yet more techniques to this book so my thanks are due to this class, including Marijke Klosterman, Fay Murray, Wendy Knight, Helen Halpin, and Brigitte Seiber. All these women, who made garments and other articles for this book, worked beyond their original brief and added their own creative ideas to mine. Unless otherwise stated, I wove and knitted the other works in this book.

ASF-Weave, in Arundel UK, where I taught myself the basics of the dévoré technique, gave me time and support and I owe them my thanks. This study was undertaken with a grant from Creative New Zealand and I am very grateful for this help.

Students in my workshops on dévoré have helped in many ways by suggesting ideas and new techniques and I will repay this help by passing on all I have learned to future workshops. Weavers and knitters are always willing to share.

My husband took most of the photographs, unless otherwise acknowledged, and these add immeasurably to this book. This is the seventh book we have done together and we are a good team.

**Anne Field**

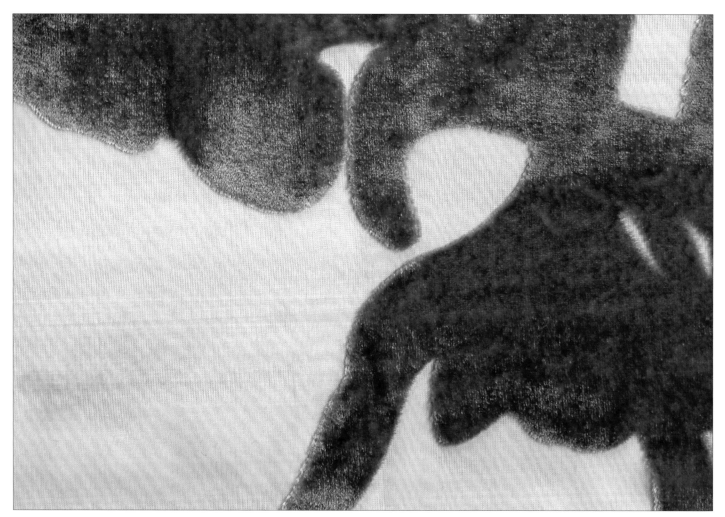

P1.1: Dévoré scarf in rayon and silk

# INTRODUCTION

Dévoré, from the French word meaning 'devour', is not new. The technique has been around for a long time. The most common use has been with silk and rayon fabrics where the rayon pile has been dissolved to leave a transparent silk background. It has also been used on silk and cotton fabric, where the cotton has been dissolved away.

There is another type of dévoré, which uses an alkali paste to dissolve protein fibres such as wool. This paste contains sodium hydroxide (caustic soda). This wool dévoré is a more complex and little-used process and will not be covered in this book. A full description can be found in *The Fabric and Yarn Dyer's Handbook* listed in the bibliography.

Considering that weavers and knitters have the freedom to make their fabric from any mixtures of yarn types, it is surprising that the dévoré technique has seldom been used on hand-woven and knitted fabrics until now. This freedom is not always possible with industrial processes. There are also many new composite yarns available on the market which weavers and knitters can use.

Dévoré is not a complex process. A substance (sodium bisulphate) is used which destroys the plant content of the fabric. Yarns that are derived from plants (linen, cotton, etc.) are mixed with those from animal or synthetic sources (silk, wool, nylon) and then mixed together in a fabric. The sodium bisulphate solution is applied to the fabric and heated. The plant content disappears, leaving behind the non-plant fibres.

I have assumed that those using this book have basic weaving, knitting and crocheting skills and understand the terms used in these crafts.

In this book, I will first describe the basic process then the variety of ways in which it can be used. I have found it a fascinating journey, first mastering the technique then applying the designs. The actual making of the fabric is not difficult; it is the designing of the pattern areas to suit the technique, which is the challenge. The yarns used in this book are listed in a suppliers' appendix at the back of the book.

## Drafts

Weaving drafts used in this book have been written using WeavePoint 6. The threading draft is in the top left segment, beginning on the right. The tie up is in the top right corner, with the treadling sequence written underneath. A black square in the draw-down (lower left segment) indicates a raised warp end.

## Abbreviations

**ch** = chain;

**dc** = double crochet;

**tr** = treble;

**inc in next st** = knit into front and back of next st;

**K** = knit;

**P** = purl;

**psso** = pass slipped stitch over;

**rep** = repeat;

**sl** = slip;

**sts** = stitches;

**tog** = together;

**yo** = yarn over.

UK crochet terminology is used (UK dc = USA sc, UK tr = USA dc)

Background. What causes dévoré? Safety precautions. Where to get the the solution. Kits. Fibres that will burn out. Fibres that will not burn out. Testing fibres. Testing mixed yarns. Yarn size. Wraps per 2.5cm (1in). Tex. Knitted and woven samples.

## BACKGROUND

Dévoré fabrics have been used in the fashion industry for many years. Originally, it was known as 'poor man's lace' and was called 'broderie chimique' in Europe because it was used to simulate machine embroidery. The main use of dévoré has been on cut velvet fabric with a pile of rayon (viscose is another name for rayon) on a silk backing. The rayon pile was burnt out leaving elaborate etched patterns on the transparent silk backing as in P1.1: Dévoré scarf in rayon and silk.

## WHAT CAUSES DÉVORÉ?

Sodium bisulphate is the burn out agent used in dévoré. This is a chemical compound, $Na_2HSO_4$, which is the by-product from the production of hydrochloric acid. Other names that sodium bisulphate is known by are monosodium salt, sodium hydrogen sulphate, sodium acid sulphate, and dry acid. The American spelling is sodium bisulfate. It is commonly used in household cleansers, silver pickling and to reduce alkalinity and PH in swimming pools.

Dévoré patterns occur when sodium bisulphate is applied to the cloth, dried, then heated. The heat process causes the sodium bisulphate to become a mild sulphuric acid, eating away at the cellulose content, which has become brittle. The cloth is then washed to remove the brittle areas. This leaves only non-cellulose treated areas in the cloth. These areas can be transparent, depending on the type and colour of the fabric.

## SAFETY PRECAUTIONS

Sodium bisulphate is an acid irritant. When mixing the raw ingredients together to make the burn out solution follow these precautions, as sodium bisulphate is a powder and can be inhaled.

- Always work in well-ventilated areas.
- Use a mask or a dust/mist respirator.
- Do not use metal or aluminium containers.
- Wear rubber gloves and plastic apron.
- Avoid contact with skin and eyes.
- Keep containers tightly closed and do not store in moist conditions or near strong alkalis.

Ready mixed solutions, such as Fiber Etch, are in a paste form; therefore, a respirator is not necessary. However, it is still an irritant. Take care to wear rubber gloves, avoid contact with eyes and skin, and work in a well-ventilated area. It is advisable to wear a mask.

## WHERE TO GET THE SOLUTION

Sodium bisulphate needs several additives to make it easier to control. It can be bought ready mixed or in a kit form. The ingredients can also be bought separately and mixed. Page 113 has a list of suppliers of the ready mixed paste (Fiber Etch) and the kits (PRO Chemical Dévoré kit, Maiwa dévoré kit, H. Dupont Devorant). The separate ingredients can be purchased at most drug stores and pharmacies.

## KITS

The kits consist of two components, the thickener and the sodium bisulphate mix. Follow the safety precautions above when mixing and using the solution and use glass or plastic mixing bowls. Three recipes follow. Full instructions are included in the kits.

## Maiwa Handprints

The kit contains a thickener and the sodium bisulphate. Mix 3 cups water with 6 $\frac{3}{8}$ tbs of P4 thickener in a blender or hand mix well. Let stand for a few hours or overnight. Measure ¼ cup of cold water and add 8 tbs of sodium bisulphate and 3 tbs of glycerine and stir well. Combine both parts and stir thoroughly. Store in the refrigerator, bring to room temperature when ready to use, and give the mixture another stir. The mixture will become thinner with time and has a shelf life of about four weeks.

## PRO Chemical & Dye

Measure 500ml (two cups) of water at room temperature. Mix 50g (⅓ cup) of guar gum in another dry container. Using a blender or by hand, start slowly adding the guar gum. Leave to stand for several hours or overnight. This is the thickener paste.

Make the burn out paste just before you are ready to use it. Measure 220ml (¾ cup) of 38° (100° F) water and dissolve 200g (½ cup) of sodium bisulphate in the water. Once this is dissolved, add 80ml (1 cup) of glycerine and the thickener paste. Mix thoroughly. Discard after three days.

## H. Dupont Devorant

Mix the reactant and paste in exact proportions: 15% of reactant powder to 85% paste. Add the reactant to the paste and stir until completely mixed. After preparation the devorant mixture must be used within eight days before it becomes too liquid.

**Fibres that will burn out**

Only cellulose (plant) fibres will disappear, as acids such as sodium bisulphate decompose these fibres. Some yarns that are coated, such as mercerised cotton, may not burn out because they have a protective coating. Fine yarns work best because thicker yarns make penetration of the burn out solution difficult, and the resultant effect may be patchy.

- Cotton
- Linen
- Rayon (a man-made fibre from wood pulp). It is also called viscose.
- Ramie
- Lyocell (a man-made fibre from wood pulp). It is usually known as Tencel™.
- Bamboo

**Fibres that will not burn out**

These are protein and synthetic fibres.

- Wool
- Mohair
- Alpaca
- Cashmere
- Silk
- Polyester
- Nylon
- Acrylic
- Lurex

P1.2: Fibres that will burn out.
Left to right: Back row: Tencel, rayon, cotton.
Mid row: dyed rayon, rayon, linen.
Front row: rayon bouclé

P1.3: Fibres that will not burn out.
Left to right: Back row: wool, lurex, alpaca.
Front row: polyester, silk, cashmere, mohair

## BURN TEST FOR FIBRES

Test for yarn content by using the burn test. Hold a piece of the yarn with tweezers and put a match to the other end. Remove from the flame and see what happens. Knitting yarns are usually well labelled but weaving yarns, which are often bought on cones in larger quantities, may be harder to analyse.

Nylon. Polyester – melts, forming a hard, uncrushable bead. Yellow flame. Burns slowly.

Wool. Silk – burns slowly, withdraws from flame. Burns in but not out of the flame. Forms a dark, crushable bead.

Rayon. Linen. Cotton – burns fast, continuing to burn and glow out of the flame. Yellow flame. Feathery residue.

## TESTING MIXED YARNS

P1.4: Slippery yarns

There are many interesting mixes of yarns on the market. Mostly, these are labelled but a test can be carried out with the burn out solution. Wrap the yarn around a piece of plastic card, a lid from an ice cream container is ideal, then apply the solution to part of the yarn. Dry with a hair dryer, place a piece of cardboard between the yarn and the plastic and a sheet of aluminium foil between the iron and the yarn, and iron with the iron on a wool setting. Then wash. You can see what part of the yarn is left. Luckily, I tested a yarn that I bought labelled as 50% wool and 50% Tencel. Theoretically, only the wool fibres should have remained, however, the yarn lost none of its fibres and, therefore, was not suitable for dévoré. Another yarn labelled as silk was actually rayon when I tested it. I should have guessed as it cost very little.

Many of these yarns, such as rayon, are very slippery and will fall off the cone. A nylon stocking pulled over the cone can prevent this. The stocking can be left on while winding off the yarn.

## YARN SIZE

The thickness of the yarn makes a difference when applying the burn out solution. Because the solution has to penetrate right through the yarn thinner yarns require less solution. Hand-knitted garments are usually thicker than woven fabric, because the knitting technique produces a slightly three-dimensional fabric. Machine-knitted cloth is usually thinner than hand-knitted because finer yarns can be knitted very quickly on a knitting machine.

## WRAPS PER 2.5CM (WPI)

A wide variety of yarns can be used with dévoré, which means that it can be difficult to size these yarns in a way they can be recognised and purchased. Many countries have different names for yarns and knitting and weaving yarns are also labelled differently. For example, a knitting yarn labelled 'double knit' in New Zealand may be called 'sports weight' in another country. In this book, I will identify the yarns by using the wraps per 2.5cm (1in) method along with their usual commercial name. This method measures the size of the yarn, regardless of the number of plies, by wrapping the yarn around a ruler for 2.5cm (1in), then counting the wraps. Do not pull the yarn tight because this makes it thinner, and make sure the yarns touch each other.

The name under which the yarns can be purchased will be given first, with the wraps per 2.5cm (1in) in brackets, e.g. Tex 110/2 (32wpi). Because the conversion from metric to imperial measurements is often clumsy, 32wpi, which is short for '32 wraps per inch', will also mean wraps per 2.5cm.

## TEX

Many yarns I use in weaving are named by the Tex system, a metric system in which yarns are described by the weight in grams of 1000 metres. Therefore, a yarn named Tex

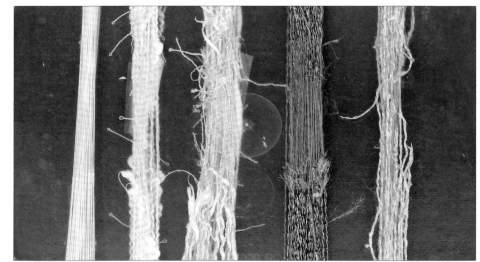

P1.5: Testing yarns mixed in the manufacturing process. From the right: Cotton/nylon. Rayon/polyester. Cotton 54%/acetate 38%/nylon 8%. Cotton 61%/polyester 16%/nylon 16%/acrylic 7%. Cotton-covered polyester

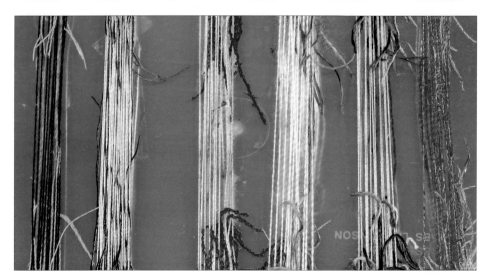

P1.6: Testing yarns mixed by hand. From the right: Alpaca/lurex/Tencel. Silk/dyed rayon. Rayon/wool. Silk/bouclé rayon. Silk/rayon. Wool/cotton

110/2 has 1000 metres weighing 110g. The no. 2 indicates the ply number. The lower the first number the finer the yarn.

## KNITTED AND WOVEN SAMPLES

Sampling is a good test if you want to determine whether the knitted or woven fabric is suitable. One reason for sampling is to test for dye fastness. Sometimes, the sodium bisulphate solution will cause the dye to run. Usually, the dye that runs into the dévoré area will wash out with the final wash and rinse, but sampling will warn you if this is going to be a problem.

Sampling will also show how various yarns react to the sodium bisulphate. I found that some of the silk yarns I used hardened after applying the solution and washing. This can be a problem if the design areas are going to be in skin contact.

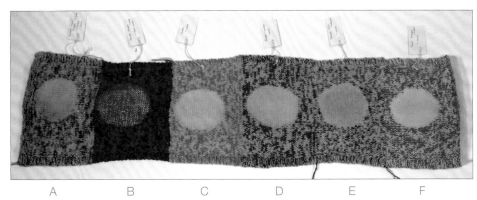

| A | B | C | D | E | F |

P1.7: Knitted Sample
Cream wool (18wpi) was twisted together with the following yarns:
A. random-dyed rayon (28wpi), lurex (64wpi) B. bouclé rayon (22wpi) and random-dyed wool (28wpi). Cream wool was not used in this sample C. cotton (20wpi) D. rayon (24wpi)
E. 10/2 Tencel (32wpi) F. susi rayon (35wpi)

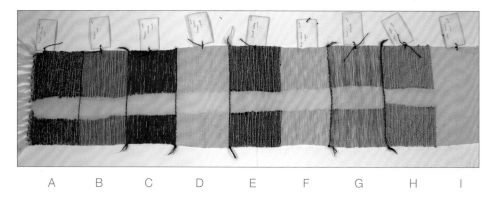

A    B    C    D    E    F    G    H    I

P1.8: Woven sample.
Warp: Tex 110/2 (32wpi) cream wool. Weft: same as the warp and twisted together with the following yarns.

- A. rayon bouclé (22wpi)
- B. rayon (24wpi)
- C. rayon chenille (16wpi). 1450 yards per pound
- D. linen (30wpi)
- E. cotton (20wpi)
- F. space-dyed Tencel (112wpi)
- G. space-dyed Tencel (112wpi), rainbow polyester (112wpi)
- H. susi rayon (35wpi)
- I. 10/2 Tencel (40wpi)

Yarn mixes: Blended yarns. Mixed yarns. Mixing the yarns yourself. Doubling stand. Spinning yarns together. Shuttles for weaving. Twist amount. Weaving the cloth. Hand knitting the cloth. Machine knitting the cloth. Weavettes.

## YARN MIXES

Two types of fibre will be used for dévoré: one that will burn out (contains cellulose fibres) and one that will not (contains protein and synthetic fibres). There are three ways these fibres can be made into yarn.

### Blended yarns

The two different types are blended together in the yarn-making process, e.g. a blend of 60% cotton and 40% wool. It is always necessary to test this type of yarn, as on page 18, to determine how much yarn is left behind after the dévoré process. I wove the sample in Photo 2.1 with a blend of 75% cotton/25% wool. I realised too late that there was not enough wool in the blend because the fabric was weak when woven. Testing the yarn first would have been a better idea.

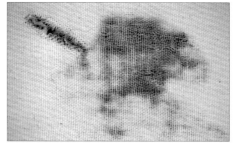

P2.1: Fabric woven with 75% cotton/25% wool

### Mixed yarns

One, two or more strands are plied together, e.g. one strand of nylon and one of cotton. One yarn can also be covered or coated in another yarn in the manufacturing process, as with cotton-covered polyester (Coats T-105 industrial thread). Again the yarn needs to be tested first, as in Photo 1.5.

### Mixing the yarns yourself

This gives the most freedom because you can mix and match to your heart's content. See Photo 1.6 for some of these mixes. Sometimes this can make the knitting or weaving challenging because you are using yarns that may be very different in composition, stretch, and smoothness. Working with a mixture of Tencel and wool is an example. Wool, unless it is pre-treated, will shrink, is fluffy and dull, and stretches. Tencel is smooth, shiny, does not stretch and will not shrink. When I first started researching the dévoré technique and used yarns such as this, I just wound them together from the separate yarn packages and knitted or wove from the resulting yarn.

Several things happened. When weaving, however carefully I worked, one yarn would gradually get longer than the other one. I would have to stop, cut the longer yarn and overlap it so both yarns were the same length again. This was a frustrating and slow process. When I washed the finished piece, sometimes the edges would have little loops where one yarn would shrink in and the other would not. When knitting, the needles would slip into the gap between the two yarns and I would end up with little loops on the back of the knitting or I would have to unpick, again, a frustrating process.

Then I remembered the doubling stand, a gadget, which prevented this problem.

## DOUBLING STAND

One cone of yarn is placed under the other cone, the yarn on the lower cone is brought up through the centre of the upper cone, and the two are wound together while applying yarn tension with the pressure of your fingers. The upper yarn is twisted around the lower yarn as you wind. This twist makes the yarns more compatible. A stool with a hole in the centre makes a suitable doubling stand, although the one illustrated is easy to make and is portable into the bargain.

P2.2: Doubling stand

The yarn can be from other types of yarn packages but coned yarn is easier on the doubling stand because it unwinds smoothly from the larger end up to the smaller end. If the yarn is in a ball, place the ball in a box to prevent the ball running away and place the box in the lower position on the doubling stand. With both yarns in balls, cut a hole in a cardboard box placed under the upper yarn and run the yarn from the lower ball through the hole and up the centre of the upper ball.

The type of yarns used can make a difference. Even with the doubling stand, two slippery yarns such as silk and Tencel wound together can end up different lengths. Wool is easier to use as one of the yarns because it is not smooth and other yarns will cling to it.

## SPINNING YARNS TOGETHER

If you are a spinner, there is another way to twist the yarns together. Check which way the yarns are twisted, then, using your spinning wheel, ply the two yarns together the opposite way to which they were originally plied. This will make the yarn more stable. Most commercial yarns are plied in an S direction, so spin them together with a Z twist.

Using a spinning wheel puts in more twist than a doubling stand, and you can control the amount of twist. Too much twist may make the yarns harsh to the touch.

## SHUTTLES FOR WEAVING

When weaving, the type of shuttle can make a difference to the amount of twist inserted. Using the doubling stand and winding the yarns on to a stick shuttle puts less twist in than winding the yarn on to a pirn (end delivery shuttle) or a bobbin (boat shuttle). A boat shuttle with two separate bobbins will allow for the different yarns to be used at the same time.

F2A: S and Z twist

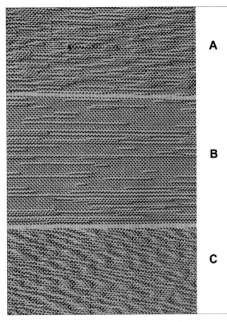

P2.3: Twist in yarn with rayon and silk
A. Wound from a doubling stand on to a pirn
B. Yarn wound from a doubling stand on to a stick shuttle
C. Yarn plied on a spinning wheel

## TWIST AMOUNT

The amount of twist inserted into the two yarns makes a difference to the appearance of the finished cloth. The yarns change from upper to lower positions as you weave or knit. High-twist yarns change positions more often. One of my weaving students decided she did not like the effect of the twisted yarns so placed the yarns on separate shuttles and placed and beat each pick separately. This proved so tedious that she soon gave up.

## WEAVING THE CLOTH
### Structure

Where the dévoré solution is applied to the cloth only part of the cloth will be left behind. Where the burn out area meets the surrounding areas the yarn that has been dissolved looks as if it has been cut. This is not noticeable if the yarns are fine but if the yarns are thick, the weave structure has long floats, or it is too open, these cut edges look untidy. They can be trimmed with sharp scissors if they are not too long.

Plain weave is the most stable structure for a dévoré cloth as the yarns intersect every second thread, as in darning. This minimises the float length and leaves tidy edges to the design areas.

Other weave structures, such as 2/2 twill where the weft goes under two/over two warp ends, can be used if the weaving is sett close enough. This will be discussed fully in Chapter Eight.

P2.4:  Edges of burn-out area

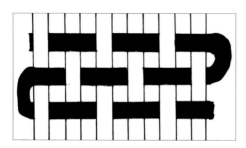

F2B: Plain weave

## Sett

The sett, the number of warp ends, and the number of weft picks (rows) to the cm (in) should allow for an almost balanced cloth in the burn out areas. This area, which is thinner than the surrounding areas, should be stable and strong. Sampling is often the best way to find out which sett to use. Testing the yarn, as on page 18, is also useful as you can then see what proportion of the yarn is left behind. Usually, it is not possible to weave an absolutely balanced cloth when the warp has one yarn, which will not burn out, and the weft has two; one that burns out and one that does not. If the same two yarns are used in the warp and weft, a balanced structure can be woven.

For example, if you are weaving with a Tencel and wool warp with the same two yarns in the weft, only the wool yarn will be left in the burn out areas. Therefore, if the two-yarn warp is sett at 16 ends per 2.5cm (1in), the burn out areas of wool will have eight ends because the Tencel has burnt out of the fabric. Eight ends may be too few and these burn out areas will be unstable as in the photo.

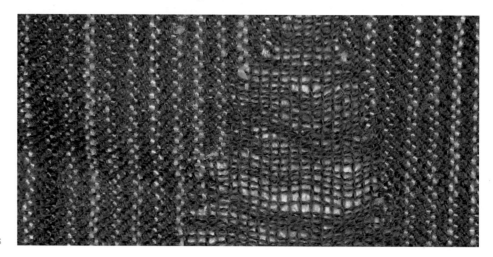

P2.5: Unstable burn out areas

However, if the sett is 32 ends per 2.5cm (1in), the burn out areas will be stable at 16 ends. However, the surrounding areas may be too rigid. A compromise of 12 ends per 2.5cm (1in) may be the answer. Sampling is the best way to test this.

Another way to determine sett, if you are weaving with a non-burn out yarn (silk) in the warp but with the two yarns (silk and a burn out yarn) in the weft, is to weave the first few picks in the yarn that will remain in the burn out areas. In the scarf described below weave for 5-6 cm (2 in) with the same silk used in the warp and do not include the fibre that will burn out. Allow for the relaxing of the tension that takes place when the weaving comes off the loom and you can judge whether the silk warp and weft area will be stable enough. If that first area is too sleazy, re-sley the reed closer and weave with more picks to the cm (in). If the test area is too firm, re-sley with a wider sett, and weave with fewer picks.

## Weaving

The easiest way to describe how to weave dévoré cloth is to describe in detail one scarf. This scarf has the burn out yarn (rayon) only in the weft.

**Warp yarn:** 20/2 silk (38wpi)

**Sett:** 20 ends per 2.5cm (1in)

**Length of warp:** 3m (3yds)

**Width:** 25cm (10in)

**Weft yarn:** One strand of 20/2 silk and one strand of random-dyed, brushed rayon (28wpi). The yarns were wound onto a pirn from a doubling stand.

**Weave structure:** Plain weave on four shafts, threaded 1, 2, 3, 4.

The cloth was woven with 20 picks to 2.5cm (1in). Make sure the beating is very even as any unevenness shows up in the burn out areas. Hem stitching strengthened the ends.

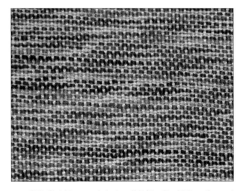

P2.6: Woven fabric. 20/2 silk (38wpi) and random-dyed, brushed rayon (28wpi)

P2.7: Hand-knitted sample. 20/2 (38wpi) silk and random-dyed, brushed rayon (28wpi)

## HAND-KNITTING THE CLOTH

It is much easier to gauge how firm the fabric should be for knitting rather than weaving. When knitting altering the needle and yarn size can change the fabric density. With weaving you have to re-sley the loom! A sample swatch is a good way to test to check the yarn and appropriate needle size. Using the same yarn as in the woven sample; 20/2 silk and random-dyed, brushed rayon, I had to double the silk yarn to knit a stable fabric. Using one strand of silk made the burn out area too thin and loose.

Knit a few rows with the silk on its own and see if that area will be stable and firm enough. If so, add the burn out yarn, in this case the random-dyed rayon, and continue knitting. If the silk knitting is too loose, change to smaller needles or thicker yarn. If it is too tight, use larger needles or thinner yarn.

A knitted structure with long floats will not give a satisfactory edge when the burn out solution is applied, as there will be long threads at the edge of the burn out areas. Stocking stitch, garter stitch, and moss stitch, are the easiest to begin with. Later, when you have more experience, you can try fancier stitches. To prevent the edges rolling with stocking stitch, knit two or three stitches on each edge in garter stitch.

In the sample in Photo 2.7 the needle size was 2¾ m (12 English) (1 US).

## MACHINE KNITTING THE CLOTH

This sample was designed and knitted by Heather Phillips on a Brother 910. As machine knitting is usually firmer than hand knitting, the background yarn was used as a single strand.

Instructions:

Cast on FNR

80sts MB, 79sts RB

Tension 5/5

Rib 120 rows

Cast off.

# WEAVETTES

These simple looms can also be used to weave fabric for dévoré. Two sizes of weavettes were used in the scarf in P2.9. The joins are decorative and the edges were finished with a crocheted stitch.

Weavettes can also be used to make small samples when trying a new yarn or in workshop situations.

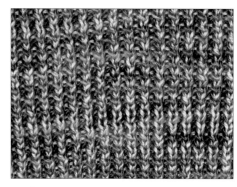

P2.8: Machine knitted sample one strand each of 20/2 (38wpi) silk and random-dyed, brushed rayon (28wpi)

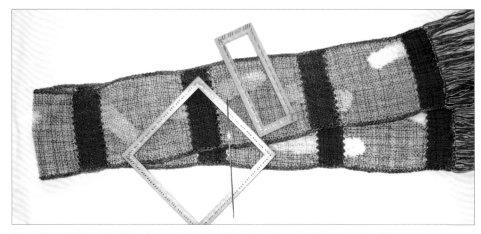

P2.9: Scarf in 110/2 (32wpi) wool and random-dyed brushed rayon (28wpi) woven on weavettes by John Mullarkey

## What you need: The process

The samples used in this chapter are those described in the previous chapter; woven or knitted with 20/2 (38wpi) silk and random-dyed, brushed rayon (28wpi). The process is basically the same whether the cloth is woven or knitted. If the yarn is oily, dirty or contains sizing, scour the cloth before beginning the process.

**What you need:**
- Sharp scissors or a craft knife and cutting board
- Pins
- Old towel
- Metre (1yd) of aluminium cooking foil
- Newspaper
- Iron
- Plastic apron
- Hair dryer (optional)
- Small glass jar
- Sheet of plastic
- Freezer paper
- Fiber-Etch or sodium bisulphate solution
- Brush
- Rubber gloves
- Mask
- Pencil and eraser

## THE PROCESS

Lay the fabric on a flat surface. The cloth may need pressing to ensure there are no wrinkles. Cut out a section of freezer paper to cover the areas which will be burnt out. Freezer paper has one shiny side, which will adhere to the cloth when it is ironed.

Draw the required design in pencil on the dull side of the freezer paper. The chapter on design will help with this. Start with a simple shape for your first work because this is easier. Also, fine detail will be lost.

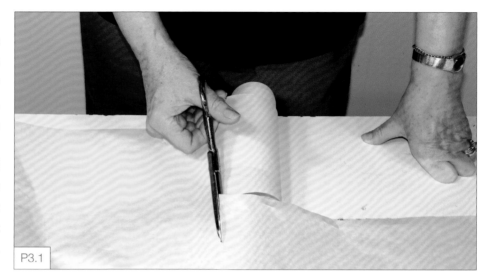

P3.1

P3.2

Cut out the shape with sharp scissors or use a cutting board and a cutting knife. Remember that the spaces in the freezer paper template will be the burn out areas.

Pin the paper template onto the cloth and iron the paper with the shiny side on the cloth and the dull side uppermost. Use a dry iron on a medium setting such as the wool setting. Make sure the edges of the template adhere to the cloth. It may be necessary with knitted cloth to press the cloth out flat first.

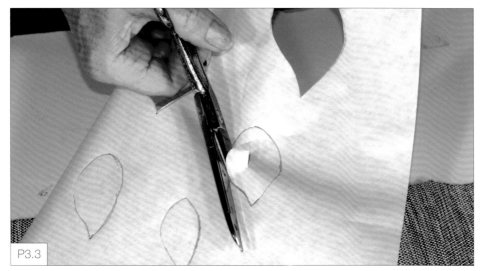

P3.3

P3.4

To protect your clothes and your skin, wear rubber gloves and a plastic apron and work in a well-ventilated room. A mask can be used. Place a sheet of plastic on the worktable and put the cloth with the attached freezer paper template on the plastic.

Use a firm-bristled brush and brush the burn out solution onto the cloth, working it in well. Brush out from the template as this prevents the solution from seeping under the paper.

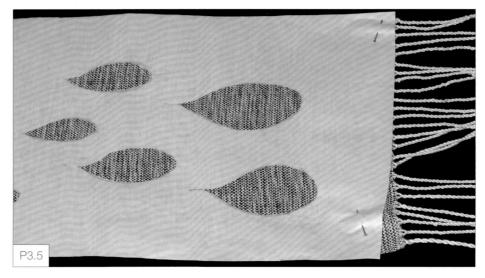

P3.5

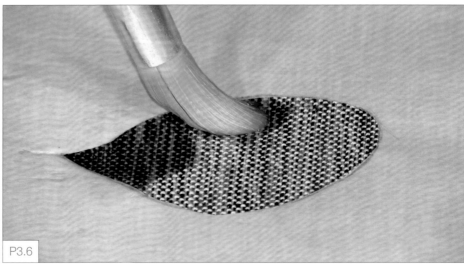

P3.6

Turn the cloth and template over, onto a clean section of the plastic and check that the solution has completely penetrated. If not, touch up these areas.

Knitted cloth, which is generally thicker than woven cloth, needs more solution to completely penetrate.

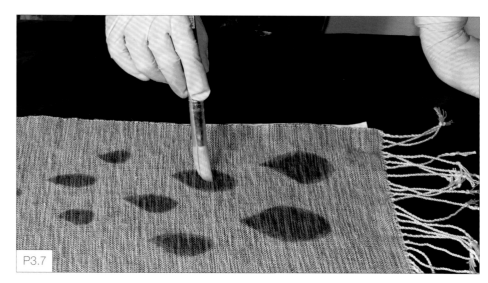

P3.7

P3.8

Leave the cloth to dry overnight. A hair dryer can hasten the process. The area where the burn out solution has been applied may change colour but because this only affects the yarns to be burnt out, this does not matter. Do not leave the solution on the cloth for longer than necessary.

When the cloth is completely dry, remove the freezer paper template, place newspaper or an old towel over the ironing board to protect the surface and lie the cloth onto the surface. Place a sheet of aluminium foil on top of the cloth and iron with the iron on dry, not steam and a setting suitable for the yarns used. I find a wool setting is suitable for most yarns. Keep the iron moving and frequently check the cloth surface. Work in a well-ventilated area. Wear a mask.

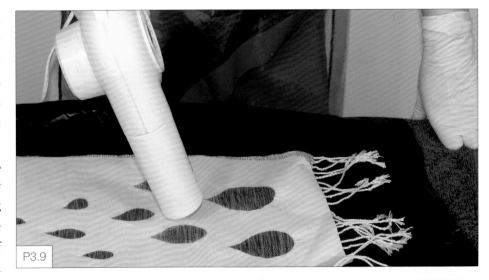

P3.9

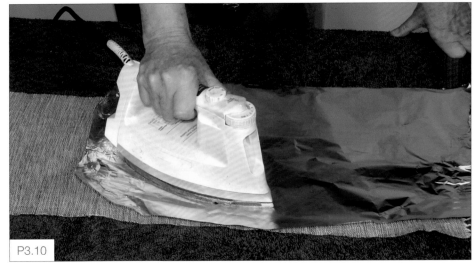

P3.10

P3.11

Iron until the surface goes pale brown. Take care not to scorch the cloth. The sodium bisulphate solution becomes a mild acid which burns out the plant content. Turn the cloth over and repeat the ironing process on the other side.

The burn-out areas become brittle and will begin to break up when scratched with a fingernail, so test for this. However, do not try to remove all the burn out fibres this way, as the fibres can be breathed in.

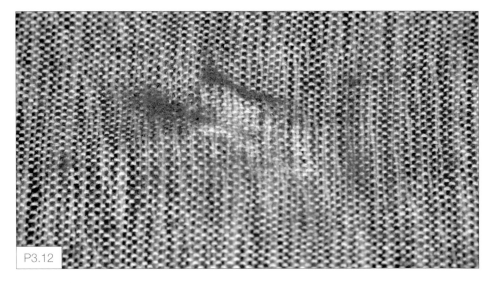

P3.12

Wearing rubber gloves wash the fabric thoroughly in warm water, rubbing gently in the burn out areas to remove all the plant fibres. If using wool and the wool is not shrink-proof, too much rubbing will cause felting. I discovered this by accident and the result can be seen on page 107. I ended up making a feature of this mistake.

Sometimes, the sodium bisulphate solution will cause the dye to run, but a rinse in soapy water and a final rinse again will usually remove the over run dye. Dry the cloth and then press while slightly damp.

If the burn out areas are incomplete, e.g. some plant fibres remain in those areas, the whole process can be repeated in those missed areas. I found that the black wool yarn used in photo 5.2A and B on page 61 and 62 made it difficult to see which places I had missed when ironing the cloth, because I could not tell when the burn out areas turned pale brown.

P3.13

P3.14

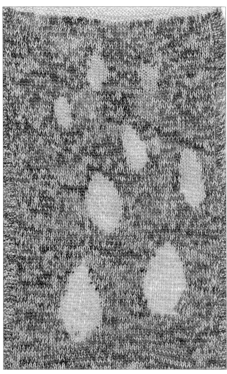

P3.15: Woven sample with dévoré pattern.

P3.16: Hand-knitted sample.

P3.17: Machine-knitted sample.

The same template was used in the machine-knitted sample as in the woven and hand-knitted samples, but with more widthways stretch in the fabric, the shapes are broader.

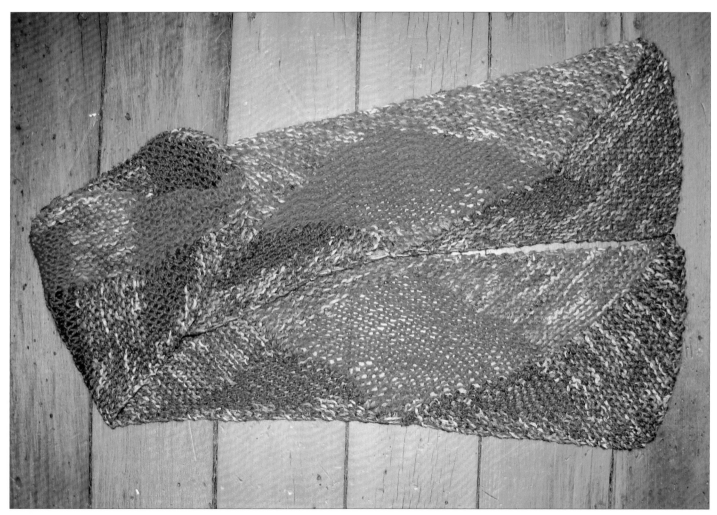

Multi-directional scarf

# 4. DYEING

Weaving: Random-dyed burn out warp. Random-dyed burn out warp and weft. Random-dyed non-burn out warp. Space-dyed non-burn out warp and weft. Random-dyed non-burn out warp and burn out weft. Random-dyed non-burn out warp and weft. Dyeing complete articles after weaving. Dyeing the burn out areas only. Random-dyed burn out weft. Commercially dyed weft yarn. Random-dyed non-burn out weft. Knitting: Random-dyed burn out yarn. Multi-directional scarf. Dyeing the non-burn out yarn. Knitting with a commercially dyed non-burn out yarn (Opal). Dyeing the non-burnout yarn after knitting.

Weaving or knitting dévoré fabric with random or commercially dyed yarns adds immeasurably to the interesting effects you can achieve with dévoré. Some of the yarns used in this chapter have been commercially dyed; some have been dyed especially for me by small production dyers and some I have dyed myself.

In weaving, the burn out yarns can be dyed, either in the warp or weft, or the non-burn out yarns can be dyed in the warp or the weft, or a combination of these four possibilities can be used. This gives a wide variety of combinations and the headings become rather cumbersome. With knitting you are usually using only two yarns and either the burn out or the non-burn out yarns can be random-dyed, or commercially dyed. With knitting you can also change the yarn combinations as you knit, whereas, in weaving, the warp yarn cannot be changed once the warp is on the loom. In both weaving and knitting, the complete article can also be dyed after the dévoré process.

Many of the effects seen in the weaving samples can be achieved by knitting, and vice-versa.

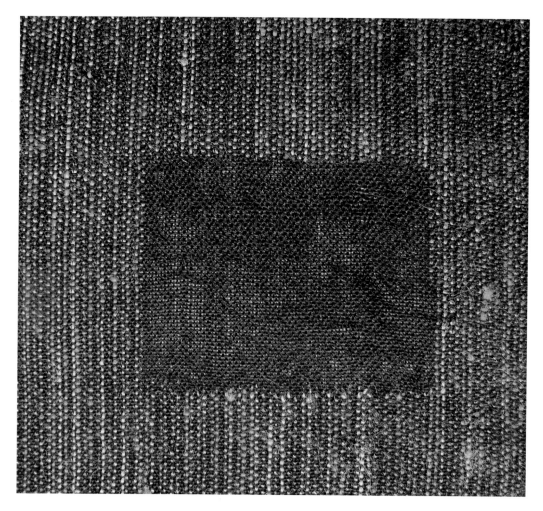

P4.1A: Random-dyed burn out warp

# WEAVING

### Random-dyed burn out warp

Two warps were needed: one, which will burn out; and one, which will not. For this example, I used a supplementary warp which stopped 2.5cm (1in) short of the side borders. This supplementary warp was the burn out, random-dyed yarn.

**Warp:** black alpaca yarn 2/28 (48wpi). Alpaca is an animal fibre and will not burn out.

**Sett:** 30 ends per 2.5cm (30epi).

**Supplementary**

**warp:** random-dyed brushed rayon (28wpi). This is the burn out fibre.

**Sett:** 15 ends per 2.5cm (12epi)

**Width:** Background: 23cm (9in).

**Supplementary:** 20cm (8in)

**Weft:** Black alpaca, same as the warp. Woven at 24 picks per 2.5cm (24ppi)

**Threading:** As the black alpaca yarn was nearly half the thickness of the rayon, the threading for the supplementary warp section had two ends of alpaca to one end of rayon as in Figure 4.1. For the plain weave border, thread with the alpaca on Shafts 1 and 2 only. For the supplementary warp section, thread following the draft in 4.1. The rayon was the pattern warp ends on Shafts 3 and 4. I used two beams on my loom for this warp, because the tension was different for each yarn. However, if the warp is no longer than 5m (5yds), both yarns can be wound on the same beam.

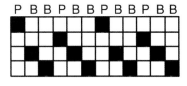

P = Pattern
B = Background

F4.1: Draft for photos 4.1A and B

P4.1B: Random-dyed burn out warp and weft

### Random-dyed burn out warp and weft

This was the same warp as in Photo 4.1A but the weft was one strand of the black alpaca and one of the random-dyed rayon woven as one weft thread.

### Random-dyed non burn out warp

**Warp:** White merino wool, 110/2 (32wpi). This warp was dyed before it went on the loom.

**Weft:** One thread of black 110/2 (32wpi) wool wound together with a thread of black 10/2 (40wpi) Tencel.

**Sett:** 12 ends per 2.5cm (1in). An allowance of about 15% shrinkage was made in the sett for this wool. A yarn of the same size that does not shrink should be sett closer.

**Width:** 25cm (10in)

**Dyeing:** I wound the warp, then dyed it, using Earth Palette dyes, which are fibre-reactive. I used the cold pad batch method where the dye was painted onto the wool, wrapped in plastic, then left for a minimum of 24 hours at a temperature of 20° C. By dyeing onto dry wool, I could control the spread of the dye. If dyeing wet wool the dye colours run into each other more. This scarf (P4.2A) was woven with a two-thread weft consisting of one thread of black Tencel and one thread of black wool. The Tencel was then burnt out. The weft yarns were wound onto a pirn using a doubling stand.

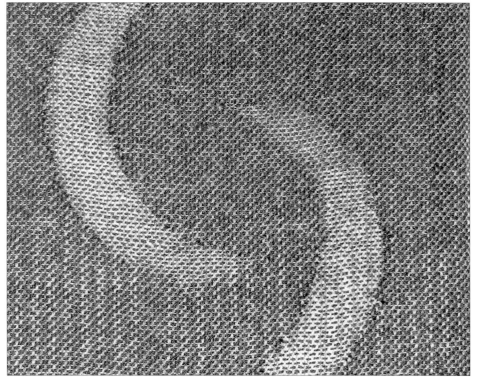

P4.2A: Random-dyed non-burn out warp

## Space-dyed non-burn out warp

**Warp:** Two different, space-dyed, 2/14 weight (28wpi) fine micron Australian wool yarns from Kaalund Yarns. Page 50 explains the difference between space-dyed and random-dyed yarns.

**Weft:** Pink wool (28wpi) and red 10/2 (40wpi) Tencel.

**Sett:** 16 ends per 2.5cm (1in).

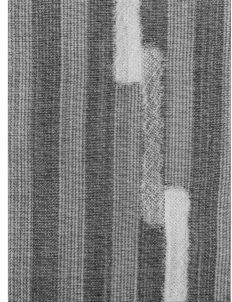

P4.2B: Striped space-dyed non-burn out warp

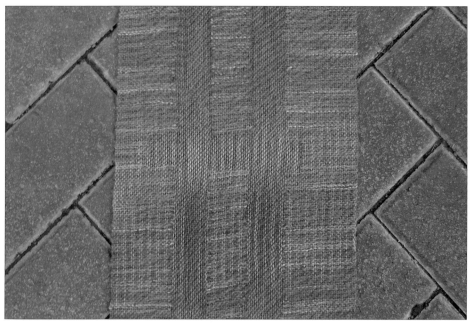

P4.2C: Random-dyed non-burn out warp

### Random-dyed non-burn out warp and burn out weft

This scarf (4.2C) was woven with the same warp as 4.2A with a two-thread weft consisting of a random-dyed rayon (28wpi) and red wool yarn (110/2 (32wpi), the same size yarn as the warp). The rayon was burnt out. A doubling stand was again used.

### Random-dyed non-burn out warp and weft

This scarf (4.2D), with the same warp as 4.2A and C, was woven with a two-thread weft consisting of a random-dyed wool (28wpi), weft together with black 10/2 (40wpi) Tencel. The Tencel was burnt out. A doubling stand was again used.

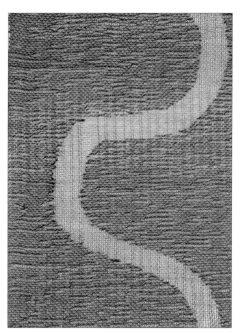

P4.2D: Random-dyed non-burn out warp and weft

## DYEING COMPLETE ARTICLE AFTER WEAVING

**Warp:** White merino wool, 110/2 (32wpi).

**Weft:** One strand of white merino, the same as the warp and one strand of grey Tencel (40wpi).

**Sett:** 12 ends per 2.5cm (1in). As this yarn shrank about 15% this was allowed for in the sett. A yarn of the same size that does not shrink would be sett closer.

**Width:** 25cm (10in)

**Dyeing:** After the scarf was woven a template was designed and applied. The dévoré solution was painted on, dried, ironed and washed. When the scarf was dry, the complete scarf was dyed with Earth Palette wool dyes painted onto the fabric. Because the Tencel weft did not absorb the dye, the dévoré wool areas took the dye completely, leaving the non-dévoré areas of Tencel and wool a paler colour. I painted the dye on this scarf by blending the colours. The dye can also be painted on to form patterns.

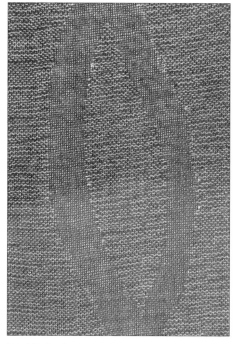

P4.3A: Dyeing complete article after weaving

In photo 4.3C, the sample was also dyed using Earth Palette wool dye. The circles became darker because these were the wool-only areas. The weft yarn dyed a paler colour because of the high cotton content. This was a much finer scarf than the scarf in photo 4.3A.

**Warp:** 56/2 (56wpi) wool.

**Weft:** One blended yarn of wool 30% and cotton 70%. (54wpi).

**Sett:** 32 ends per 2.5cm (1in).

P4.3B: Dyeing the fabric

## DYEING THE BURN OUT AREAS ONLY

**Dyeing:** The scarf was woven with the same yarns and instructions as for the scarf in 4:3a. After weaving, the template was applied and the dévoré solution painted on. The scarf was then dried, ironed, washed and then dried again. Rather like the colouring-in I did as a child, I carefully painted the dye onto the dévoré areas only, trying hard not to go over the edges. The Earth Palette dyes were made into a thick solution to prevent them spreading over the edges. A thinner solution will allow a blurred edge between the design and the background. Make sure the scarf is completely dry before applying the dye if you want clean edges.

P4.3C: Dyeing the complete article

P4.3D: Dyeing the burn out areas only

P4.3E: Painting on the dye

P4.4A: Commercially dyed weft yarn

Random-dyed burn out weft (see photo 3.14)

This is the scarf shown in Chapter Three, page 36, with a silk warp and a two-thread weft of random-dyed rayon and silk.

## COMMERCIALLY DYED WEFT YARN

This scarf was woven with a very fine dyed Tencel weft. The yarn was commercially dyed with regular intervals of colour changes. It is not possible for large commercial dye houses to random-dye yarn in irregular colour patterns, as I can do with my smaller amounts. When I dye yarn, I lay out the hanks then paint a bit of dye here and there. Yarn produced by large commercial dyers has regular colour changes which, when woven, give a pattern as seen on this scarf.

Usually this type of commercial dyeing is called 'space dyeing' and is achieved by dip dyeing, printing or flatbed dyeing. With this commercially dyed Tencel, I could not tell how the pattern was forming, until I had woven several cm (in). The width of the article will change the pattern. I applied the burn out solution without a template, following the shapes made by the dyed weft.

**Warp:** 56/2 (56wpi) wool and 2/20 cotton as one end.

**Weft:** Space-dyed Tencel (112wpi) and 56/2 wool (56wpi).

**Sett:** 24 ends per 2.5cm (1in).

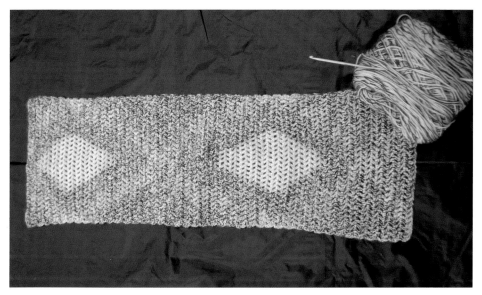

P4.4B: Sample crocheted by Wendy Knight

This is another sample, crocheted in space-dyed cotton and wool, which shows the colour pattern caused by the regular colour changes in the dye. Usually the pattern does not show up until several cm (in) have been crocheted. It always seems a bonus when this happens to me, as the colour pattern only emerges when the width is right for the space dyed sequence and I cannot tell this in advance.

The crochet pattern was worked with a size 2mm hook as follows. 1tr, 1ch, mesh crochet (1dc, 1ch mesh in USA).

## Random-dyed non burn out weft

**Warp:** 140/2 Tex (26wpi) possum 40%, merino 50%, silk 10% yarn.

**Sett:** 12 ends per 2.5cm (1in). The warp yarn had a high shrinkage of about 25-30%, so this is allowed for in the sett.

**Weft:** One strand of Kaalund fine micron space-dyed Australian wool, 2/14 weight (28wpi) and one strand of blue 10/2 (40wpi) Tencel. The Kaalund yarns are space-dyed but the repeated sequence is not always obvious, thus, a random effect is produced.

P4.5: Random-dyed non-burn out weft.

## KNITTING
Random-dyed burn out yarn

The sample in Photo 3.16 was knitted with cream silk and random-dyed rayon. Knitting instructions are on page 28.

## MULTI-DIRECTIONAL SCARF

This scarf was knitted with the triangle shapes alternately knitted in blue and red wool together with the space-dyed bamboo as the burn out yarn. The dévoré design was repeated in the larger triangles. This multi-directional scarf pattern is included with the kind permission of Karen H. Baumer © 2003. Mathew Hesson-McInnes has given permission to use his ending of the scarf, which gives both ends the same appearance.

**Materials:** It takes approximately 185m (200yds) to make a 15cm (6in) wide scarf. For this scarf, one strand of wool (10wpi) and one strand of the space-dyed bamboo (9wpi) were knitted together. They were not twisted together first.

**Terms: Inc.** = knit into the front and back of stitch.

**SSK** = slip next two stitches individually as if to knit, put tip of left needle into slipped stitches and knit them together.

**SKP** = slip one as if to knit, K1, pass slipped stitch over.

P4.6: Multi-directional scarf

Because these yarns were thick I had to use a lot of the burnout solution and push it well into the knitted fabric. I also had to trim with scissors some of the longer bamboo threads at the dévoré edges. The scarf was heavy and scratchy when the knitting was complete. To make the scarf light and comfortable, the dévoré areas are large, removing much of the bamboo yarn.

## INSTRUCTIONS

Cast on 1 stitch.

**Row 1:** Inc. into stitch (2sts).

**Row 2:** Inc. into first stitch, K to end (3sts).

Repeat Row 2 until one side edge of your triangle (i.e. not the "live" edge on the needle) is as wide as want your scarf. Now start your short row sections.

### Short Row Section

**Row 1:** Inc., SSK (or SKP throughout, your choice), turn.

**Row 2:** and all even-numbered rows: Knit.

**Row 3:** Inc., K1, SSK, turn.

**Row 5:** Inc., K2, SSK, turn.

**Row 7:** Inc., K3, SSK, turn.

Continue in this manner, increasing by one stitch in every odd-numbered row between the inc. and the SSK. (You will not actually need to count because you will always be SSK-ing the two stitches on either side of the gap that forms from your turn on the previous row.) Work until you have SSK-ed the last two stitches of the row.

**Next row:** start over at row 1 of the Short Row Section.

Continue working Short Row Sections until your scarf is almost as long as you want it. Once you have completed your final Short Row Section, proceed as follows:

Work as with the previous triangles until half of the stitches are on the right needle and half of the stitches remain on the left needle. Instead of starting each garter stitch ridge with an increase, start the ridge with a decrease (i.e. K1, K2tog). Continue to work the decrease in the "middle" of the row, as before, and after making this second decrease, both needles will have the same number of sts. When 6sts remain, work as follows:

**K1, K3 tog:** turn, K2.

**K3 tog:** turn, K1.

**K2 tog:** cut yarn and pull through last remaining loop.

Add a fringe if desired.

### Dyeing the non-burn out yarn

This sample (P4.7) was knitted with Heritage Hand-painted Millington 45% wool and 55% mohair (10wpi) yarn and grey 10/2 (40wpi) Tencel. A strong colour contrast is needed between the two fibres to emphasise the design.

### Knitting with a commercially dyed non-burn out yarn (Opal)

Opal yarn is used in this sample. It is a 75%, superwash wool, 25% Polyamide yarn (20wpi), which will not burn out. The space-dyed pattern is such that bands of Fair Isle alternate with plain bands when knitted. The width of the bands depends on the width of the knitting. This wool is usually used for sock knitting. This sample was knitted with one strand of black 10/2 (40wpi) Tencel and one strand of Opal on size 2.5m (12- English, 1- American) needles.

P4.7: Dyeing the non-burn out yarn

P4.8: Knitting with a commercially dyed
non-burn out yarn

## DYEING THE NON-BURN OUT YARN AFTER KNITTING

P4.9: Dyeing after knitting

In this sample photo 4.9, knitted with one strand of white wool (16wpi) and one of green 10/2 (40wpi) Tencel, the circle pattern in dévoré was repeated in the dyed design. The dye used is Earth Palette wool dye. Over-dyeing is very useful when you have slightly scorched the wool when ironing the dévoré area, as I did in this sample. The wool areas taking the dye a darker colour made for an interesting effect. The Tencel and wool areas, however, were lighter as the dye did not take on the Tencel yarn.

P5.1A: Scarf. Machine-knitted by Heather Phillips

Shape. Machine-knitted scarf. Over-all design. Shoulder shawl pattern. Contrast: colour, size. Light. Sources for designs. Tracing and photocopying a design. Designing without a template.

I am a self-taught weaver, who learned the practical side of weaving before I considered the design part. I learned from books, other weavers and short workshops. My learning was spasmodic as I picked up knowledge wherever I could. In the beginning, I was doing my best to fit it in with the demands of a young family and limited resources. With no art background, it took me years before I felt confident with the design and colour elements of my work. This chapter is a resource to help those knitters and weavers who feel the same as I did.

Dévoré fabrics are not complex and the weaving and knitting is straightforward. It is the patterns and designs made when the cellulose yarns are removed from the fabric that make the difference between beautiful and boring. The positive and negative spaces play a big part in these finished designs as we begin with a template with the positive areas removed. It is also important to think of the fabric when designing. Fine fabric, with many threads close together, enables more complex patterns to be designed. Thick fabric, with fewer threads to the cm (in), will lose definition if the design is too detailed. If you are not sure how much detail will show up on the finished work, do a sample first before starting anything major. Knitting or weaving small samples and then making small templates and applying the dévoré solution can save major headaches later.

## SHAPE

The shape of the finished article is a good starting point when considering the dévoré design. For example, a scarf is a long, narrow piece of fabric, only the ends showing when it is worn. The piece around the neck may not be seen at all because it is squashed. Therefore, a design at each end may be appropriate as in P5.1A

P5.1B: Paua wrap Woven with rayon/
polyester yarn (32wpi). Pieces of paua shell
decorate the fringes

## MACHINE-KNITTED SCARF

Instructions for machine-knitting the scarf in P5.1A. The scarf was knitted on a Brother 910 machine.

**Yarn:** 2/18 black wool. 20/2 Tencel.

Put the fine knit bar in.

Both yarns together double e-wrap cast on 130sts.

Change the yarn feeder in the sinker plate to the plating yarn feeder.

Feed plating yarn (wool) in plating yarn section.

Put the main yarn (Tencel) in main yarn section.

Tension 2.

Knit 800 rows.

Cast off, using both yarns together.

Dévoré the scarf, then sew the long ends together in centre back of scarf. Sew short ends together. Add fringe if wanted.

A wrap, which is wider than a scarf, allows more of the centre section to be shown when worn. Both these scarves and wraps may need the design to be reversed at one end, so that, when worn, the design is viewed the same way up, as in photo 5.1B. I have had the yarn used in this wrap for years and can only make a guess at its composition. I think it has a core of polyester plied with two strands of rayon. Photo 1.5 shows the results of the testing I did with this yarn.

Designing garments or accessories to be worn on the body is different from designing work for an exhibition and I find it difficult to design work for both purposes. The wrap in Photo 5.2A looked great in an exhibition where it was hung at right-angles to the wall. There, the whole design could be seen at a glance. However, on a body the design changes completely as only sections of it are seen at a time as in Photo 5.2B.

P5.2A: Black/red wrap-full length. Woven with black 110/2 (32wpi) wool and red cotton (40wpi) Photographer John Hunter

P5.2C: Over-all design

P5.2B: Black/red wrap when worn.
Photographer: John Hunter

## OVER-ALL DESIGN

This scarf has a design which covers the entire scarf. Because there are large areas of dévoré, the scarf is very light and flexible. The design consists of irregular all-over shapes. These shapes do not change the design when the scarf is worn, as happens with the design in P5.2A and B.

**Warp:** 2/30Nm Tencel/wool (48% Tencel, 52% wool) (28wpi).

**Weft:** same as the warp yarn with a 2/20 (30wpi) space-dyed cotton as the second weft yarn.

**Sett:** 24 ends per 2.5cm (1in).

**Structure:** plain weave.

The Tencel content of the Tencel/wool yarn used in the warp and weft was slower to burn out than the cotton yarn and remains as an outline in the dévoré designs. This shadow effect, although unintentional, was very attractive.

Some shapes are easier than others to dévoré. Most woven cloth is all vertical and horizontal lines and knitted cloth is similar. Therefore, straight edges to the dévoré patterns are better defined than sharp curves. In Photo 5.3, I first tried making smaller circles inside the larger circles but the inner circle was not clear. A small square gave me a better outline.

**Shoulder shawl pattern in basket weave** (P5.3). With kind permission from Beverley Francis. **Materials and required gauge:** Use a combination of fine 2-ply animal and plant fibre yarns which knit at a firm tension of 6sts and 8 rows per 2.5cm (1in) over stocking stitch on a size 3.75mm (8 Eng, 5 American) circular needle. The example in Photo 5:3 was knitted in 2-ply merino wool in royal blue and a random-dyed rayon (28wpi). **Pattern:** Using wool only on 3.75mm circular needle cast on 270sts. Use yarn doubled. Knit 10 rounds garter stitch. (Remember when knitting in the round to do garter stitch means to purl alternate rounds.)

P5.3: Shoulder shawl knitted and designed by Beverley Francis in blue  wool together with random-dyed rayon (28wpi). Photographer: John Hunter. Instructions begin on page 63

Break off one thread of the wool yarn and add in the rayon, using one thread of each together. Divide the 270sts into groups of 27 stitches. Stitch markers can help to establish the pattern.

[K first 27sts then P next 27sts.] Repeat a round. This gives 10 squares in alternate knit and purl.

Continue as set for 5cm (2in) from start of pattern rows. Decrease one stitch each side of each square in pattern as follows: K2 tog, knit across square, then K last 2 tog before the start of the purl square, P2 tog, purl across square then P last 2 tog, repeat around. Continue in pattern for another 5cm (2in). On last round decrease 3sts across the top of each square as follows: K2 tog, K10, K2 tog, K9, K2 tog, P2 tog, P10, P2 tog, P9, P2 tog. Repeat around. 220sts.

On the next round purl all the knit stitches and knit all the purl stitches. Work in pattern for 2.5cm (1in) then decrease as before one stitch each side of each square. Work another 2.5cm (1in), then decrease one stitch each side of each square. Work a final 2.5cm (1in) before decreasing 3sts across top of each square as before. 150sts.

On next round, change again and knit the purl stitches and purl the knit stitches. Work as set in pattern for 2cm (1½in) then decrease one stitch at each side of each square as before. Work another 2cm (1½in), repeat decreases then work a final 2cm (1½in). On last round, decrease 3sts at the top of each square as before. 80sts.

Break off rayon yarn and add in another strand of wool. If wished, beads can be pre-strung on this strand to knit in about every 3rd to 4th stitch around base of neckline. Garter stitch for 8 rows then decrease one stitch for every square before casting off.

If wished, beads can be added on the cast-on round by crocheting around in double crochet about one bead for every 3 stitches. This adds weight to the fine yarns used.

Wash and block to 'flatten' pattern.

## CONTRAST

### Colour

The contrast between the dévoré and background areas is important. This contrast can be achieved with the use of colour. The black background and the dyed yarns in the sample in Photo 4.1A and B are more noticeable because the contrast is so high. Also, a black background makes the colours glow. The same random-dyed rayon, used as the weft in Photo 4.2C is not as obvious. If you want subtle effects, use colours that are similar in value and hue. However, if the colours are too subtle these effects may not be seen until they have a light source behind them.

The knitted top in photo 5.4 is effective because the shiny cream rayon yarn was different from the dull wool yarn in the pattern area in both colour and texture. When

P5.4: Knitted top. With permission from the author, Marianne Isager, this pattern was adapted from her book, `Knitting out of Africa'. The pattern is 'Congo', Page 36. This top was adapted and knitted by Margaret Wilson. The wool used was a merino yarn with 18wpi.
Photographer: John Hunter

P5.5: Cotton-covered polyester (T-105 44wpi) window hanging. Inlaid design woven in wool. Sett 36 ends per 2.5cm (1in)

P5.6: Shoulder cape, designed and knitted by Billee Mutton in a cotton/acrylic blend. Photographer: John Hunter

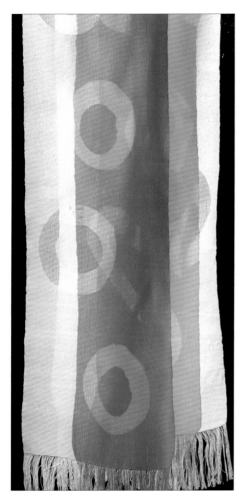

P5.7: Triple banner. Warp and weft cotton-covered polyester T-105 (44wpi), sett at 30 ends per 2.5cm (1in)

P5.8: Mosaic pattern from page 189 'Textile Designs' book'

P5.9: Wrap, with 10/2 (40wpi) Tencel hand-knitted cables by Lynne Nicholls. The centre panel was machine-knitted by Heather Phillips in 10/2 Tencel (40wpi) and wool (28wpi). Photographer: John Hunter

The knitted top in Photo 5.4A and B is effective because the shiny cream rayon yarn was different from the dull wool yarn in the pattern area in both colour and texture. When the rayon was burnt out, there was a contrast between the dévoré and the surrounding squares. Because this top had an intricate knitted design, the colours were kept to a minimum; cream rayon, and two shades of blue. The dévoré design was also kept to simple squares similar to the knitted squares. Because the garter stitch pattern created an uneven surface it took a lot of the dévoré solution to penetrate the wool.

### Size

Another contrast is between the thickness of the background areas and the dévoré designs. In the dévoré sections, some of the yarn will be burnt out and this area will be thinner than the surrounding areas. These areas can also be transparent as in Photo 5.5. In the hanging in 5.5 the same woven inlaid design was reproduced in the dévoré design but moved up and over to echo the woven design. The inlaid wool design is raised and the transparent areas appear to recede. Fig 8.1 gives the pattern draft for this inlaid weaving.

The contrast in the knitted shoulder cape in photo 5.6 comes from the contrast in the size of the two yarns used, not from the colour. Because the dévoré design is transparent, the colour comes from the garment worn underneath.

P5.10A: Tracing a design

## LIGHT

Much of the dévoré effect in fabric is best seen with light shining through. Therefore, garments that move away and out from the body, show up the dévoré designs well. Scarves and wraps are ideal in lightweight fabrics.

P5.10C: The finished design. Woven in 2/20 silk (38wpi) and 10/2 Tencel (40wpi) at 20 ends per 2.5cm (1in)

P5.10B: The template applied to the cloth

P5.11: Enlarging a shape

# TRACING AND PHOTOCOPYING A DESIGN

Being able to use the freezer paper both as a template and as tracing paper is a very useful aid in design. The paper is fine enough that most designs can be seen through it.

The finished design, although based on the tulip pattern on page 67, of '*Textile Designs*', was adapted to fit the shape and size of the scarf. I also made the design more formal than in the original.

Photocopiers are also useful design tools as the original designs can be enlarged or reduced. Remember that fine detail can be lost so look carefully at the original design and take out any fiddly bits. In my first experiments with designs, I used some overlapping circles and squares. Without using a liquid resist (this technique is covered on page 73), or a fabric pen (page 84) I could not separate the overlapping shapes and the design was lost.

## DESIGNING WITHOUT A TEMPLATE

The dévoré solution can be brushed directly onto the fabric without using a template. This will leave an irregular edge instead of a straight line and this effect can be used in a design when the aim is an edge which gradually blends into the surrounding fabric. This was done on the scarf in photo 4.4A, where the pattern the space-dyed yarn made while weaving was used as a base for the dévoré shapes. Photo 5.12 shows the edge of such a brushed design. This type of irregular edge suits less formal and stylised designs.

P5.12: Brushed design. Woven with 2/20 silk (38wpi) and random-dyed rayon (28wpi)

# 6. RESISTS

Liquid resists. Stitched resists. Bound or knotted resists.

A resist is anything that prevents the burn out solution from penetrating the fabric. The freezer paper used in the preceding chapters is a resist. In this chapter, we will explore other types of resist. Again, it is important to remember that the amount of detail in a design depends on the fineness and texture of the cloth.

Freezer paper templates give a clear and well-defined design outline. Most of the resists described in this chapter give an uneven outline which may suit less formal designs. Many of the techniques used for shibori dyeing can be used in dévoré.

## LIQUID RESISTS

These paint a line onto the fabric, preventing the burn out solution from penetrating the cloth. The burn out solution is then applied, dried, ironed, then the resist is washed out when the fabric is washed to remove the burnt out fibres. The resist solution needs to be a clear, water-soluble liquid, which can be ironed, which rules out several wax compounds used in batik fabrics.

One satisfactory resist I have used is the colourless Kontur-mittel by Marabu. This resist comes in a tube with a fine nozzle for application. Most of these resists are used in silk painting and can be purchased from shops that supply silk painters.

Fabrics woven or knitted in smooth, fine yarns will provide a flat surface which is necessary for the application of the resist. In knitted fabrics, the smooth, even side of stocking stitch is an easier surface to paint with the burn out solution than the more textured underside. Garter stitch with both sides uneven makes it difficult to apply the solution so that it penetrates completely.

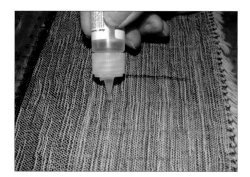

P6.1A: Applying the resist

P6.1B: Leaf pattern using a liquid resist. Warp: 56/2 (56wpi) wool. Weft: Fine Tencel (112wpi) and silk (84wpi) yarn

P6.2A: Stitched resist, before applying the burnout solution

The resist must penetrate through to the back of the fabric so some pressure is necessary, as it is not possible to turn the fabric over and repeat the resist on the other side without distorting the line. Again, experiment before undertaking a project. Drawing a line first with tailor's chalk will help, as does a steady hand. The resist spreads as it dries. The veins in the leaf shape in Photo 6.1B were the finest I could manage even although the fabric itself was very fine.

Follow the instructions that come with the resist solution. Apply the resist then let it dry naturally or with a hair dryer. If the resist line can be seen when it is dry apply the dévoré solution up to the line.

If the line cannot be seen, paint the solution over the complete dévoré surface. Then dry, iron and wash out the dévoré solution as usual.

## STITCHED RESISTS

Another method of preventing the burn out solution from penetrating the fabric is by stitching the fabric. This is done in tie-dyeing, but the main difference with dévoré is that we do not soak the fabric but paint the dévoré solution on.

The red fabric in Photo 6.2A and B was woven in plain weave with a fine white 56/2 (56wpi) wool warp and a weft of two yarns; the same wool as the warp and red 10/2 (40wpi) Tencel. The threading was a straight draw on eight shafts. Every 10cm (4ins) a Tencel weft pick was woven by lifting every 8th warp end, causing the gathering thread to float over 7 ends. If you have a four-shaft loom lift every 4th warp end but this will give you tighter gathers. This gathering thread was pulled and knotted when the weaving was removed from the loom, and before the burn out solution was applied across the gathers. If the gathering thread is pulled very tight, the dévoré solution will not penetrate as much as if the gathering is loose. The pattern is indistinct and random. When knitting, the same effect can be achieved by running some stitching threads across the fabric after knitting and pulling them tight, as in the blue machine knitted fabric in photos 5.2A using wool and Tencel.

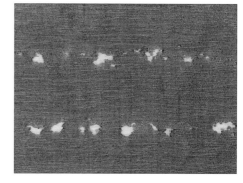

P6.2B: Stitched resist, finished

The dévoré solution is painted across the gathered rows. The amount of solution applied will determine the size of the irregular shapes.

## BOUND OR KNOTTED RESISTS

The fabric is knotted or tied with thread that will not burn out, such as nylon. Remember that in shibori, where this technique is frequently used, the complete fabric is immersed in the solution. With dévoré, we are painting the solution on so penetration of the cloth is not as easy. Marbles were used in this sample but other objects such as beads and buttons can be placed in the cloth at intervals and tied in as in photo 6.3A. The samples were woven and knitted using the same yarns as in photos 6.2A and B. To prevent the burn out solution spreading too much, I cut small holes in a plastic sheet and pulled the tied marbles through before applying the solution with a brush as seen in Photo 6.3B. If you want a more spread-out design, do not use the plastic sheet. The fabric was left to dry overnight. The ties and marbles were then removed and drying was completed with a hair dryer. The cloth is ironed and washed in the usual manner.

The fabric can also be knotted at intervals, and then the dévoré solution painted over the knots. Both these techniques will leave irregular shapes.

P6.3A: Bound resist, using marbles

P6.3B: Plastic cut to allow the tied areas to be painted

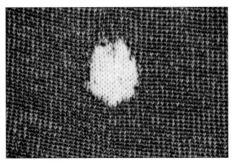

P6.3C: Finished sample, knitted

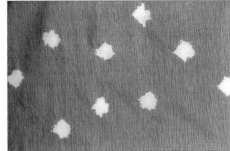

P6.3D: Finished sample, woven

Fabric paints. Pastel dye sticks. Fabric crayons. Fabric pens. Transfer paints.

Dyeing, as described in Chapter Four, adds colour through the fabric. Painting or printing on the fabric will usually cover only one side of the cloth. If this technique is used for articles where only one side is seen, such as cushions, this does not matter. If used on a scarf, where both sides will be seen at once, the design may be repeated on the reverse as well.

There are many types of fabric paints, inks, crayons and pastels that can be used on fabric. Craft shops are the main suppliers of such fabric colourings. Most of these colours are set by applying heat after application. Follow the instructions enclosed with your particular fabric paints. Also many of these colourings work only on certain fabrics so check this carefully. A trial run on a sample often saves disappointment later. The following colourings all left the fabric soft and flexible after application and ironing.

More than one type of colour can be added to a piece of fabric but my advice is to keep it simple.

## FABRIC PAINTS

The dévoré patterns in P7.1A were completed first, then a new template in freezer paper, using the same shape, was applied to the non-pattern area. The fabric paints were brushed on and left to dry. When dry the samples were ironed to set the paint. On the reverse side some of the paint showed through. This can be re-painted if necessary. The paint can be thinned with up to 25% of water but too much water will make the paint run under the templates and blur the shapes. The brushes can be cleaned in water.

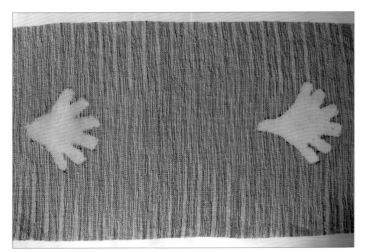

P7.1A: Sample woven with the dévoré pattern added

P7.1B: Applying fabric paints

P7.1C: Dévoré pattern repeated in fabric paints

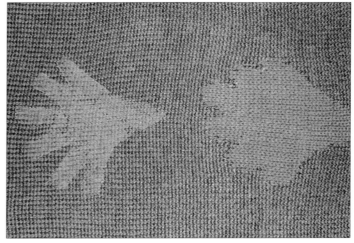

P7.1D: Sample machine knitted with the dévoré pattern added

## Woven Sample

In P7.1A, B, C the fabric sample was woven as follows:

    **Warp:** 2/30Nm Tencel/wool (48% Tencel, 52% wool) (28wpi).

    **Weft:** same as the warp for one yarn with a 2/20 (30wpi) space-dyed cotton as the
        other yarn.

    **Sett:** 24 ends per 2.5cm (1in).

**Structure:** plain weave.

In photo 7.1D, the sample was knitted with 110/2 (32wpi) wool and R100Tex/2 Tencel.

**Structure:** Plating (see instuctions for plating on page 61)

Because the knitted fabric is thicker than the woven fabric the paint remains on the surface and does not penetrate the fabric.

In photo 7.1E, the fabric paints were applied without a template and were watered down so they ran out of the dévoré area. The warp was white 110/2 (wpi) wool and yellow Tencel (150 Tex/3. Sett at 16 ends per 2.5cm (1in).

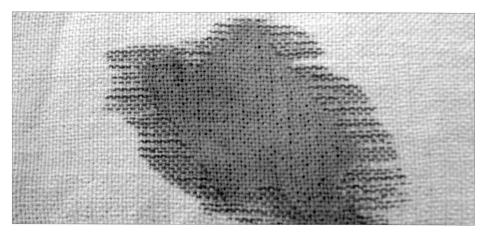

P7.1E: Sample woven by Helen Halpin

In photos 7.1F and 7.1G, the samples were knitted by Marijke Klosterman in stocking stitch, with wool and Tencel yarns.

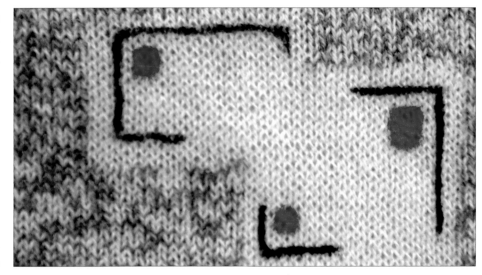

P7.1F: Hand knitted sample painted with fabric paints

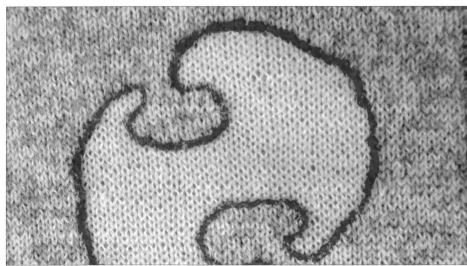

P7.1G: Outlined design in fabric paints

## Woven Sample

In photo P7.2A and B the sample was woven as follows:

**Warp:** 2/30Nm Tencel/wool (48% Tencel, 52% wool) (28wpi).

**Weft:** same as the warp for one yarn with a R150 Tex/3 Tencel as the other yarn.

**Sett:** 24 ends per 2.5cm (1in).

**Structure:** plain weave.

P7.2A: Fabric sample woven with the triangle dévoré design added

P7.2B: Painted triangle added to make a star design

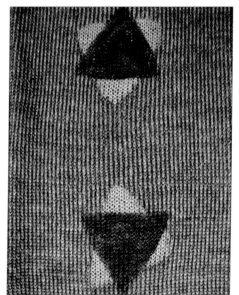

P7.2C: Fabric sample knitted with the star design added

### Knitted Sample

P7.2C sample was knitted with the same yarns and structure as in P7.1D. Again, the paint did not penetrate the fabric.

In photos 7.2B and C, the template was shifted to make overlapping stars with the fabric paint. When dry, the reverse was painted to match the front.

## PASTEL DYE STICKS

This is an easy way to colour fabric. You can draw sharp lines or smudge and layer the colours. One or both sides can be coloured.

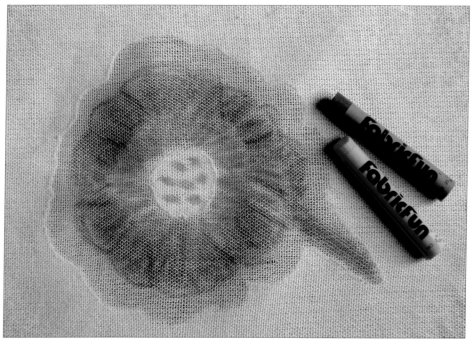

P7.3A: Design coloured with pastel dye sticks

## Woven Sample

In P7.3A the fabric sample was woven as follows:

**Warp & weft:** T-105 cotton-covered polyester (44wpi)

**Sett:** 36 ends per 2.5cm (1in)

**Structure:** plain weave

# FABRIC CRAYONS

These are similar in use to the pastel dye sticks but require more pressure to colour the fabric. It was not possible to use the crayons on knitted fabric because this fabric is too soft and flexible.

P7.3B: Design coloured with pastel dye sticks on knitted sample

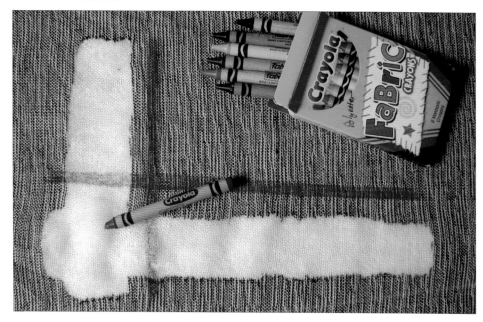

P7.4: Colour applied with fabric crayons

## Woven Sample

You will notice in P7.4 that it is harder to get a straight woven edge to the design in vertical lines than it is with horizontal lines with the dévoré technique.

In P7.4 the sample was woven as follows:

**Warp:** 2/30Nm Tencel/wool (48% Tencel, 52% wool) (28wpi).

**Weft:** same as the warp yarn for one yarn with a 2/20 (30wpi) space-dyed cotton as the other yarn.

**Sett:** 24 ends per 2.5cm (1in).

**Structure:** plain weave.

# FABRIC PENS

Again these are heat set after use to set the colours. These pens can make thick or thin lines depending on the size of the point. These pens are ideal where you want an outline or to add fine detail to a dévoré design. For example, fine veins can be added to a leaf design as in 7.5A.

The knitted sample used the same yarns as in P7.1D. The sample in P7.5B and C was woven as follows:

**Warp:** 56/2 (56 wpi) wool and 2/20 cotton.

**Weft:** 56/2 (56 wpi) wool and fine space-dyed Tencel (112wpi)

**Sett:** 24 ends per 2.5cm (1in).

**Structure:** plain weave.

After the circles were made in the dévoré technique, the outline was drawn on with a black fabric pen, then ironed to set the colour. Before the outline was added, it was not possible to see that the design was two interlocking circles as in P7.5B. With the outline, the design became clear.

P7.5A: Leaf design on knitted fabric

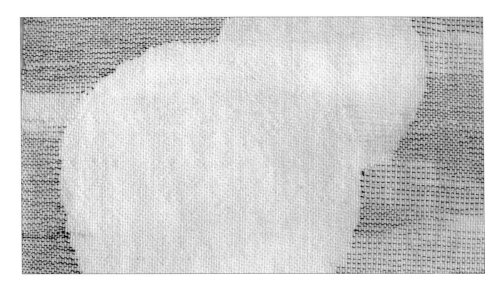

P7.5B: Original dévoré design

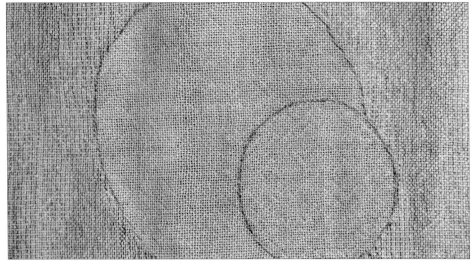

P7.5C: Woven fabric with outline in fabric pen

## TRANSFER PAINTS

These are not as readily available as the paints described earlier in this chapter but I will list two suppliers at the back of the book. The instructions state that transfer paints can only be used on synthetic fabrics but they can also be used on cotton, although the colours are paler. This means they have a more limited use than the paints described earlier in this chapter. T-105 cotton-covered polyester yarn, which makes an excellent dévoré fabric, produces very interesting effects when transfer paints are used. The dévoré areas, where only the polyester remains, are darker than the cotton/polyester areas.

P7.6A: Test piece with transfer paints

The paints are brushed onto plain, non-absorbent paper. Make sure the paint is applied evenly. Newsprint or a sheet of newspaper with a clean sheet on top is placed on the ironing surface and the fabric to be painted is placed on this underlay. Place the painted paper face down onto the fabric and press with a dry iron set to an appropriate setting. Iron back and forth with a downward pressure for about a minute to transfer the paint from the paper to the fabric. You can gently life the paper at one edge to check. Brushes can be cleaned with water. Again, check the specific instructions for your brand of paint. The paper pattern is reversed so remember this when designing.

It is sensible to do a test piece first. This test can check the colours, which may appear different from the colour in the container and will change depending on the fabric used. Also you can see how much paint is necessary. In my test piece in P7.6A, I applied the paint unevenly. After the first, uneven transfer I moved the paper and pressed it again with the iron, without applying more paint. Each application gets paler. You can also see that the dévoré stripes, where only polyester remains in the cloth, are darker than the cotton/polyester areas.

This sample and my test piece were woven with the same yarns and structure as in photo P7.3A.

P7.6B: Transfer painted crosses

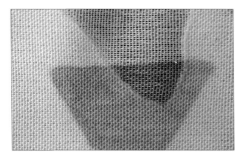

P7.6C: Triangle design in transfer paints

P8.1: Detail of 5.5

Woven embellishments: Inlaid weaving. Theo Morman technique. Collapse weave. Supplementary warp. Twill weave. Linked weft, Rosepath, Summer and winter Stripes. Knitted patterns. Textured knitted patterns. Crochet. Knitted Strips. Adding Lurex yarns. Felting Embroidery.

There are many techniques that can be added to the dévoré cloth to make it three-dimensional or to change the cloth structure in some way. It is important that these embellishments become part of the cloth and the dévoré design, not just additions that overwhelm or obscure the original design.

## WOVEN EMBELLISHMENTS

### INLAID WEAVING

Removing the plant content of a fabric makes it three-dimensional to some degree. Adding woven shapes to the cloth surface will enhance this effect. These shapes can be laid over the dévoré shapes as in photo 5.5 where the inlaid woven pattern was echoed by the dévoré design.

The woven inlaid design was woven on a plain weave background of T-105 (44wpi) cotton-covered polyester. The pattern weft consisted of three strands of fine wool (each 28wpi). The colour order of these three strands changed from dark to light from the lower end of the hanging to the upper end. This colour change was caused by replacing one strand of the three-strand yarn at a time.

With an eight-shaft loom, every third pick ties down the pattern weft by lifting Shafts 3 and 7 alternately as in Fig 8.1. With a four-shaft loom the pattern weft can be tied down on Shafts 3 and 4, and the pattern weft has shorter floats than in the eight-shaft version.

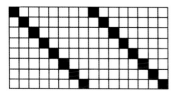

B = Backgound
P = Pattern

F8.1: Draft for inlaid design

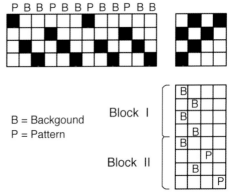

B = Backgound
P = Pattern

Block I

Block II

F8.2: Draft for Theo Morman technique

# THEO MORMAN TECHNIQUE

This is similar to the inlaid design above, but the pattern area remains on the surface of the weaving, giving a higher profile than the inlaid design.

The woven and the dévoré designs are the same shape. Thread following Fig 8.2. The warp on Shafts 1 and 2 and the background weft was a black alpaca 2/28 (48wpi) yarn, sett at 30 ends per 2.5cm (1in). The warp yarn on Shafts 3 and 4 was a random-dyed brushed rayon (28wpi) sett at 15 ends per 2.5cm (1in). The same warp and weft yarns were used in the sample in Photo 4.1A.

The background was woven with the black alpaca weft in Block 1. The design squares in the Theo Morman technique were woven as in Block 11 with the random-dyed rayon as the pattern weft and the black alpaca as the background yarn. The pattern weft was held down by the ends on Shafts 3 and 4 and only covers the design areas.

P8.2: Sample woven in Theo Morman technique

# COLLAPSE WEAVE

In one of my classes, I took an over-twisted wool yarn by mistake instead of another fine wool yarn. One of my students used this as a weft together with a yarn that burnt out. Her design featured a vertical stripe; another piece of luck because if she had made horizontal stripes the fabric would not have collapsed.

My last book was on collapse weaves. Collapse cloth puckers and pleats after the tension is released and the cloth is washed. One of the reasons this collapse happens is because high-twist yarn is used as a weft instead of a balanced yarn. To see this happen in the dévoré design was an amazing accident. Because the fabric in the dévoré areas had this over-twisted weft and was finer than the surrounding areas the pleating was quite pronounced. The background areas, with the Tencel and wool weft could not collapse because the cloth was heavier.

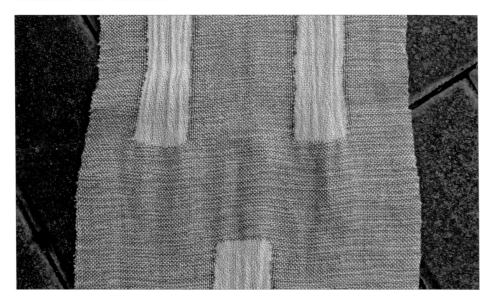

P8.3: Collapse cloth. Warp: cream 2/20 (38wpi) silk, sett at 20 ends per 2.5cm (1in). Weft: green 10/2 (40wpi) Tencel and 1/40 (64wpi) over-twisted wool

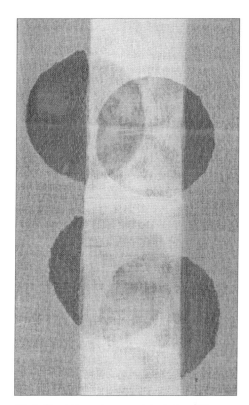

P8.4: Supplementary warp hanging. Warp and weft: T-105 cotton-covered polyester. Sett at 30 ends per 2.5cm (1in)

## SUPPLEMENTARY WARP

The use of supplementary warps allows two overlapping panels to be woven, one wider than the other. These panels were joined together every few cms (ins.) unlike the banners in Photo 5.7. I wound two warps for this window hanging and then wound them onto separate beams on the loom. The background warp was 23cm (9in) wide and the supplementary warp was 10cm (4in) wide. The yarn was white cotton-covered polyester (T-105 44wpi); a yarn that will not yellow in strong sunlight. It became transparent in the burn out areas when the cotton was burnt out. This yarn is an industrial sewing thread and behaves very much like linen on the loom. It does not stretch or shrink and is unforgiving if a warp end is pulled loose in the shed while weaving. Thread Block A for the one-layer areas. Thread Block B for the two-layer area.

The supplementary warp remained on the surface for most of the woven length, only taken under the background warp for four picks to attach the two layers. Because this was plain weave, only four shafts were used. Block I was woven for 20cm (8in) then the layers were exchanged by weaving Block II once. Weave with a tight warp tension.

To burn out the pattern, the hanging was laid on a table so the background was uppermost. The stencil with the circle design was applied to this background layer. Sheets of aluminium foil were placed between the layers and the burn out solution painted on the background layer. The aluminium foil remained between the layers until the burn out areas were dry and ironed. The work was then washed and dried. The layers were then reversed and the same process done with the supplementary warp. With overlapping circles the two transparent areas shimmer as the light shines through both layers.

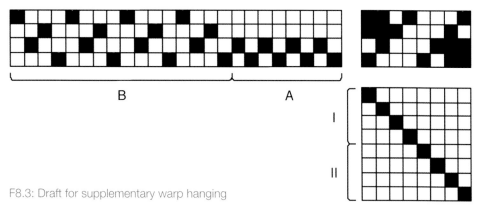

F8.3: Draft for supplementary warp hanging

## TWILL WEAVE

Plain weave is the usual weave structure for dévoré fabric because the over one/under one yarn structure leaves stable edges between the dévoré pattern and the background areas. Twill weaves, with less frequent intersections, have floats over two or three threads which can give an untidy edge to the pattern areas.

However, if the twill weave is fine and firm, 2/2 twills can be woven, as in photo P8.5A. This scarf was woven as follows:

**Warp:** 110/2 (32wpi) wool

**Weft:** 56/2 (56wpi) wool with a second weft yarn of grey 10/2 (40wpi) Tencel.

**Sett:** 16 ends per 2.5cm (1in)

**Structure:** 2/2 twill

The weft was beaten firmly and stripes of 110/2 (32wpi) wool and 2/20 (30wpi) space-dyed cotton were added at intervals. Because there are less intersections in 2/2 twill, compared with a plain weave, the edges of the dévoré designs have longer threads showing and are more obvious than in a scarf woven in plain weave.

P8.5A scarf in 2/2 twill, woven by Amy Norris

In areas that are not burnt out, other weave structures can be woven as a contrast because the structure will not affect the pattern edges. In Photo 8.5B, the scarf was woven in 2/2 twill between the design areas. Because the weft picks were woven with a twisted, doubled weft of black Tencel and wool the usual twill diagonal line was blurred. Notice how the twill areas have pulled in more at the selvedges than the plain weave areas, which is usual when these two weave structures are combined in one work.

Other weave structures can be woven in the sections in between the design areas but take care that the work does not become 'busy'. If you want the design area to be dominant the background is best left plain.

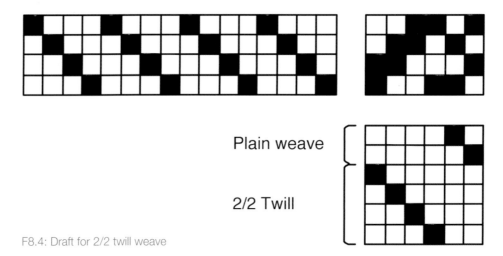

Plain weave

2/2 Twill

F8.4: Draft for 2/2 twill weave

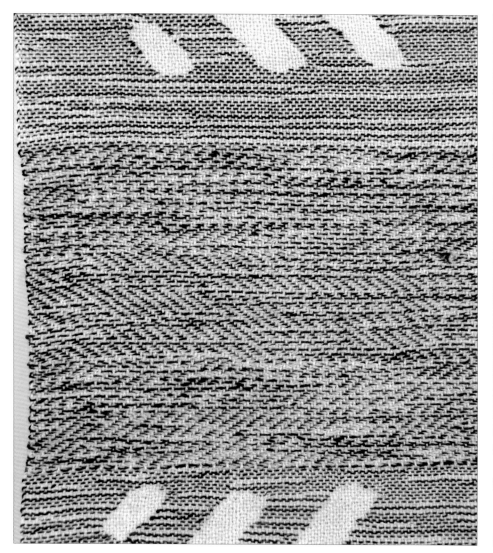

P8.5B: Scarf woven by Alison Francis. Warp: cream 110/2 (32wpi) wool, sett at 16 ends per 2.5cm (1in). Weft: cream 110/2 wool and black 10/2 (40wpi) Tencel

P8.5C: Detail of 8.5A

P8.6 Linked weft design

## LINKED WEFT

This is a simple weave structure which adds areas of colour to woven fabric. These coloured areas can then have a dévoré design included.

This linked weft scarf is woven in 2/2 twill weave on a straight draw threading as in the draft in F8.4. Weave the body of the weaving with a doubled weft as the pattern areas also have a doubled weft. To weave the linked areas, take the shuttle with a single background weft throught the shed to the opposite edge. Link this background weft through the pattern yarn and return the shuttle back to the other selvedge dragging the pattern yarn through the shed. Adjust the position of the background and pattern wefts until they are in the required position. The pattern weft does not need a shuttle and can remain on a cone or in a ball. The shed remains open for both passes of the shuttle. Then beat.

In photo 8.6, the background weft was a 150 Tex/2 possum/merino yarn in black. The pattern yarn was a blue 10/2 (40wpi) bamboo yarn. The pattern areas can be woven from either the right or left of the weaving. The squared dévoré design was added before the fabric was washed.

## ROSEPATH

This weaving pattern has the longest float over three threads so it is possible to add a dévoré design if the sett is close enough. In photo 8.7A the warp was fine alpaca (70% alpaca, 30% silk), sett at 30 ends per 2.5cm (1in). The edges of the design do have some longer ends but the fabric is stable. The small diamonds that are formed by the rosepath pattern are echoed by the dévoré design.

Block 1 of the treadling is the background weft (tabby) which is woven as alternate picks between each pattern shot. In the body of the weaving repeat Block 11 as required with the tabby binder. When you have finished weaving the complete article, repeat the first pattern pick in Block 11 to close the diamond. The scarf was woven as follows.

**Warp:** alpaca/silk Nm 2/28 (48wpi)

**Weft:** alpaca, as in the warp and 16/2 (24wpi) cotton

**Sett:** 30 ends per 2.5cm (1in)

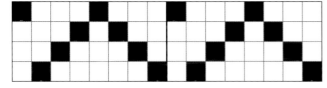

P8.7B: Detail of dévoré design

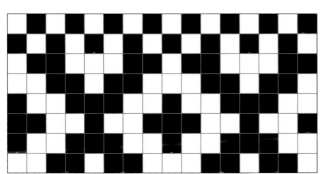

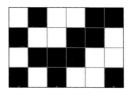

P8.7A Rosepath scarf

F8.6: Rosepath draft

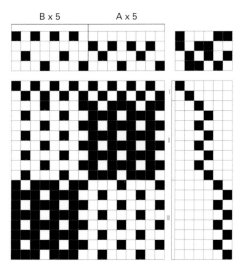

F8.7: Summer and winter draft

# SUMMER AND WINTER

This is another weaving pattern that has the longest float extending only over three threads, making it suitable for dévoré.

**Warp:** Jaggerspun Zephyr 50% superfine merino wool, 50% silk; 5040 yards per pound (28wpi).

**Weft:** Background weft, same as the warp. Pattern weft, Bambu 7, 100% bamboo 2100 yards per pound.

**Sett:** 20 ends per 2.5cm (1in)

**Threading:** Follow the draft in F8.7. Each block contains 40 ends.

**Weaving:** The background weft (tabby), added in between each pattern pick, is woven on shafts 1 and 2, 3 and 4, which is different from most other tabby picks, as shown in Block 1.

P8.8A: Summer and winter pattern. Woven by Amy Norris

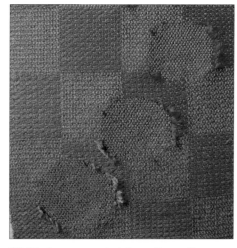

P8.8B: Summer and winter pattern with dévoré design in circles. Woven by Amy Norris

The weft is treadled in the 'alternating manner'. That is, for Block 11, shafts 1 and 3 alternate with shafts 2 and 3, with the tabby added between each pattern pick. This block is woven for 40 picks. Then Block 111 is also woven for 40 picks, alternating shafts 1 and 4 with shafts 2 and 4, again adding the tabby picks as before.

When the dévoré design is added, one image is superimposed on another. In photo P8.8B, the edges of the design in the bamboo yarn have not been trimmed. It is interesting to note that the long edge threads occur in the solid red blocks which have the longest floats. However, if you want tidier edges, trim the edge threads with sharp scissors.

## STRIPES

The burn out yarn does not have to cover the entire woven area. Warp with a non-burn out yarn such as wool. Weft stripes can be woven with two yarns acting as one weft yarn. One yarn is the same as the warp and the other weft yarn is the burn out yarn in a contrasting colour. In between these stripes, weave sections with the warp yarn only. The dévoré design covering both the stripes and the plain background will be broken up and interesting effects can be designed. This is similar to the design in the knitted sample in photo 8.16.

## KNITTED PATTERNS

Patterns can also be knitted in between the design areas as described for twill weaves in woven cloth, as in photo 8.9. The shrug in photo 8.9 has the dévoré in the plain knitted areas where the heart shapes show to their best advantage. The length of the shrug is 1.5m (5ft), width 38cm (15in) and it was knitted and crocheted with a mixture of textured cottons and wools. The length is then folded in half and the sleeve edges sewn together.

Plain stocking stitch can be embellished as in photo 8.10 by using the burn out solution to remove some of the threads. This sample was knitted with one thread of silk

P8.9: Shrug, designed, knitted and
crocheted by Billee Mutton.
Photographer: John Hunter

and eight threads of Tencel. The burn out solution was applied to one vertical row of the knitting, breaking the eight Tencel threads, which remain as vertical fringes outlining the dévoré area. This pattern area is left with horizontal silk threads.

## TEXTURED KNITTING PATTERNS

Many different knitting stitches can be used to create interesting textures when used in conjunction with dévoré.

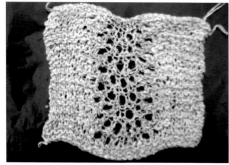

P8.11: Feather and Fan sample, woven by Fay Murray in linen and silk noil

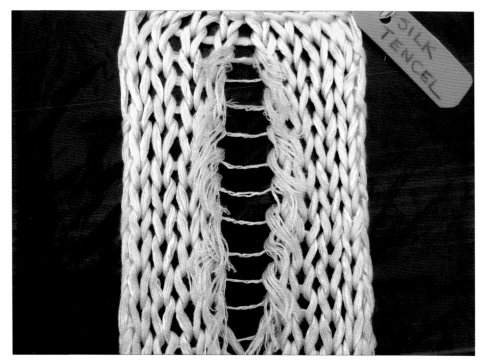

P8.10: Knitted design by Marijke Klosterman

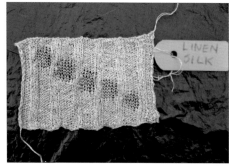

P8.12: Ribbed (purl 3, knit 2) sample knitted by Marijke Klosterman in linen and silk

**Instructions for knitting photo 8.13**

Cast on multiple of 3 sts, plus 2 extra

**Row 1:** Knit

**Row 2:** P2, *K1, P2, rep from * to end

Rep rows 1 and 2 once

**Row 5:** K2, *inc in next st, K2 rep from * to end

**Row 6:** P2, *K2, P2, rep from * to end

**Row 7:** Knit

**Row 8:** As row 6

**Row 9:** K3, *inc in next st, K3, rep from * ending last rep K2

**Row 10:** P2, *K3, P2, rep from * to end

**Row 11:** Knit

**Row 12:** As row 10

**Row 13:** K4, *inc in next st, K4, rep from *ending last rep K2

**Row 14:** P2, *K4, P2, rep from *to end

**Row 15:** Knit

**Row 16:** As row 14

Continue increasing in this way in every 4th row.

P8.13: Sample knitted by Wendy Knight in white 8 ply knitted cotton-ribbon wool

P8.14: Upper pattern in sample knitted in lime green rayon bouclé and wool. Lower pattern knitted in black wool and rayon bouclé. Both knitted by Wendy Knight

**Instructions for knitting lower black and tan section and lower part of the white and green section.**

## Broken Rib

Cast on multiple of 4sts, plus 3 extra.

Row 1: *K2, P2, rep from *to last 3 sts, K2, P1. Rep this row.

**The white and green section with zig zags.**

## Zig Zag Eyelet Pattern

Cast on multiple of 8sts, plus 3 extra.

Row 1: K2, *yo, sl 1, K1, psso, K3, K2tog, yo, K1, rep from *to last st, K1.

Row 2: and alt rows: K2, purl to last 2 sts, K2.

Row 3: K3, *yo, sl 1, K1, psso, K1, K2tog, yo, K3, rep from * to end.

Row 5: K4, *yo, sl 1, K2tog, psso, yo, K5, rep from * ending last rep K4.

Row 7: Knit

Row 8: As row 2

Rep rows 1 to 8

P8.15: Sample crocheted by Brigitte Seiber in bamboo and wool

# CROCHET

Crochet can also be used to make an interesting cloth to dévoré. The following sample may give you some ideas of how to embellish crocheted fabric. See also photo 4.4B in an earlier chapter.

This sample was crocheted as follows: There are an even number of chains.

**Row 1:** miss 3 ch, 1 tr in next ch, * 1 ch, miss 1 ch, 1 tr in next ch, rep from * to end.

**Row 2:** (1 dc, 1 ch) in first tr, 1 tr in 1 ch sp*, 1 ch, miss 1 tr, 1tr in 1 ch, rep from* working last tr in top of turning ch.

Repeat row 2

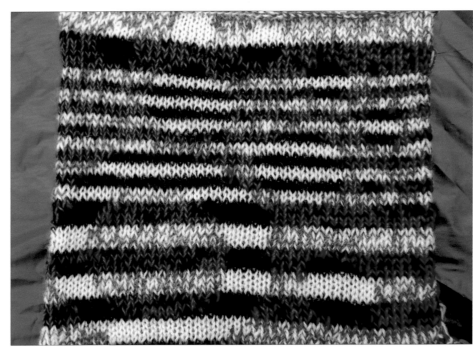

P8.16: Knitted stripes by Marijke Klosterman

# KNITTED STRIPES

The sample in photo 8.16 was knitted in stocking stitch in white and black stripes with rayon as the burn out yarn.

This is similar to the woven stripes described earlier in this chapter. The sample in photo 8.17 was knitted with the plain background in stocking stitch knitted with 2-ply wool (16wpi). The stripes were knitted with the same yarn and a dark blue 10/2 (40wpi) Tencel.

# ADDING LUREX YARNS

Lurex yarns add a sparkle to your weaving or knitting and because lurex does not burn out it will show in both the design and background areas. A little goes a long way. Some lurex yarns are scratchy so check this before using them in garments that are worn next to the skin. (Photos 8.18 and 8.19).

P8.17: Knitted stripes

P8.18: Sample knitted with lurex yarn

P8.19: Scarf woven by Janie Gummer.
Warp: 110/2 (32wpi) cream wool, sett at
16 ends per 2.5cm (1in). Weft: 110/2
(32wpi) cream wool, grey 10/2 (40wpi)
Tencel and lurex

## FELTING

Many of the creative ideas I have come from mistakes and this scarf (photo 8.20) was no exception. I was weaving a scarf for 'Handwoven' for their black and white issue (January/February 2007). The scarf was woven with a black 110/2 (32wpi) wool and white 8/2 (36wpi) Tencel warp, sett at 24 ends per 2.5cm (1in). The weft was the same two yarns as the warp. When I was washing out the Tencel in the dévoré circles I rubbed too hard and felted the wool in one circle. The 110/2 wool I use is shrinkable so this is easy to do. Luckily, I had woven two scarves, so I was more careful with the second one. I nearly threw away the one with the felted circle then decided to make a feature of it. I felted all the wool circles by heavy rubbing in warm soapy water. This caused the background to pull and gather around the felted areas. Washing the scarf in the full cycle of the washing machine would probably have the same effect.

### Felted Cloth

When teaching in the UK in 2007, I had a clever felter in one of my dévoré workshops. Anne Willitts uses commercial felt and one of her felt samples which she brought to class to experiment on was made from a wool/vicose blend. By burning out the viscose content, fine designs could be made. These neck pieces are the result of further experimentation. The felt was dyed after the dévoré was finished, using disperse dyes. The dyes were first printed on newsprint and then the colour was transferred onto the felt in the heat press. An ordinary iron can be used.

P8.20: Felted scarf.
Photographer: John Hunter

P8.21A & B: Felted neck pieces by Anne Willitts. Photographer Riq Willitts

## EMBROIDERY

Burning out some of the fibre content of cloth removes some of the yarn. Embroidery does the opposite; it adds yarn. Take care that this embellishment becomes part of the design, not just an add-on to the cloth surface. The two works in photos 8.22 and 8.23were the result of a careful collaboration with Barbara Johns. The wrap in photo 8.22 was embroidered with the raised wings of the butterflies worked in needle lace, (using double brussels stitch and french knots).

P8.22: Butterfly Shadows wrap. Warp: cream 56/2 (56wpi) wool, sett at 30 ends per 2.5cm (1in). Weft: green 10/2 (40wpi) Tencel and 56/2 wool. Embroidered design by Barbara Johns. Photographer: John Hunter

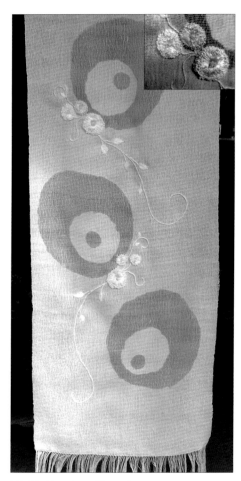

The hanging, Clematis, was worked in the following:

**Flowers:** pistil stitch, french knots and beading.

**Leaves:** raised fishbone stitch.

**Stems:** chain stitch.

Outlining the dévoré design with stitching can add both texture and colour. The knitted blanket in Photo 7.13 has fish shapes outlined in the same rayon (26wpi) as the burn out yarn in the knitting.

The squares are surrounded by garter stitch borders in the blue wool only and this also emphasises the dévoré fish.

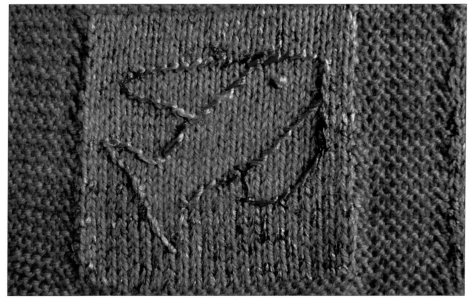

P8.23: Hanging. Clematis.
Warp and weft: T-105 (44wpi) cotton-covered polyester. Sett at 30 ends per 2.5cm (1in). Embroidered design by Barbara Johns

P8.24: Fish blanket, designed and knitted by Kathy McLaughlin

# BIBLIOGRAPHY

## BOOKS

Brackmann, Holly: *The Surface Designer's Handbook.*  Interweave Press, USA. 2006.

Cole, Drusilla, ed. *1001 Patterns.* A. C. Black, London

Isager, Marianne: *Knitting out of Africa.*   Interweave Press. 2005.

Kendall, Tracey: *The Fabric and Yarn Dyer's Handbook,* Collins & Brown Ltd. 2001

Lee, Iris: *Fabric Etching,* Dragon Threads, 2000.

Meller, Susan and Joost Elffers: *Textile Designs. 200 Years of Patterns for Printed Fabrics arranged by 'Motif, Colour, Period and Design'*, Thames and Hudson, London. 1991.

Patterns are available free of royalties and permission with the purchase of the digital version, TEXTILE DESIGNS DIGITAL from info@design-library.com

## MAGAZINE ARTICLES

Brackmann, Holly: *Shibori Meets Dévoré.*  Handwoven, January/February, 2002.

Brackmann, Holly: *Handwoven Dévoré.* Handwoven, September/October, 2004.

Field, Anne: *Dévoré for Handwoven Scarves.* Handwoven January/February, 2007.

# SUPPLIERS

These suppliers have kindly allowed their names to be listed.

Fiber Etch (R) Fiber Remover. This is the registered trademark of Silkpaint Corporation, 18220 Waldron Drive, Waldron, MO 64092, US.  www.silkpaint.com. Fiber Etch is also available from the sources listed below. This is the dévoré solution used throughout the book.

## Australia
- Silksational, 220 Woodpark Road, Smithfield, NSW, 2164 Australia. www.silksational.com.au

## Canada
- Maiwa Handprints Ltd, 6-1666 Johnston St, Granville Island, Vancouver, BC V6H 3S2, Canada. www.maiwa.com

## New Zealand
- Creative Craft Supplies, 20 Elliot St, Johnsonville, Wellington, New Zealand. sales@creativecraftsupplies.co.nz

## United Kingdom
- Fibrecrafts, Old Portsmouth Road, Peasmarsh, Guildford, Surrey, GU3 1LZ, UK. www.fibrecrafts.com

## USA
- The Plaid Company. www.plaidonline.com

# DÉVORÉ KITS

Detailed instructions for using these kits are on page 12.

## Canada

- Maiwa Handprints Ltd, 6-1666 Johnston St, Granville Island, Vancouver, BC V6H 3S2, Canada. www.maiwa.com

  This company supplies a kit containing P4 thickener and Sodium bisulphate. The other additive, glycerine, is available at most pharmacies and drug stores.

## France

- H. Dupont SAS, 31 Rue de l'Étoile du Martin, 44600 Saint Nazaire, France. contact@h-dupont.com, www.h-dupont.com.

  This devorant kit is packaged in two containers; the reactant and paste. It can also be purchased in Australia from Passion De Soie, 5/145 Peel St, P. O. Box 936, Kew, Victoria, Australia. Silk and Threads, 175 Waterfalls Rd, Mt Macedon 3441, Australia.

## United Kingdom

- Fibrecrafts. See address on page 113

## USA

- PRO Chemical & Dye, P.O. Box 14, Somerset, MA 02726, US. www.prochemical.com.

  The kit contains 100 grammes sodium bisulfate, 25g Guar gum, 2oz glycerine, 1oz Synthrapol, together with instructions.

# FREEZER PAPER (REYNOLDS)

## New Zealand
- Creative Craft Supplies, 20 Elliot St, Johnsonville, Wellington. sales@creativecraftsupplies.co.nz

## United Kingdom
- Creative Grids, The Hollows Farm, Leicester Lane, Desford, Leicester. LE9 9JJ www.creativegrids.com (look under foundation paper). Most quilting shops supply freezer paper.

## USA
- Most supermarkets stock Reynolds Freezer paper.

# DYES
- Earth Palette Cold Dyes, Post Office Box 40, Gladstone, South Australia 5473, Australia. www.earthpalette.com

# LIQUID RESISTS
- Kontur-mittel Marabu outliner used in silk painting.
- Marabu GmbH & Co. KG, Asperger Str 4, D-71732 Tamm, Germany. www.marabu.com. Also available from Hands Ashford NZ Ltd. www.hands.co.nz.

# TRANSFER PAINTS
- G & S Dye and accessories Ltd. 300 Steelcase Rd, Unit 29, Markham, Ontario, L3R2W2 www.gsdye.com - Also available from Fibrecrafts. See address on page 113

## YARN SOURCES

A wide range of yarns, other than the ones listed, are also available from the following suppliers.

Australia

- Glenora Weaving and Wool, P0 Box 9 Gerringong, NSW 2534, Australia. www.glenoraweaving.com.au (Possum/merino yarn, high twist yarn, 110/2 merino)
- Christine's Yarns, 39 Warratta Rd, Killarney Vale NSW 2261, Australia. www.christinesyarns.com.
- Kaalund Yarns, PO Box 17, Banyo, QLD 4014, Australia. www.kaalundyarns.com.au (Space dyed fine Australian wool).

New Zealand.

- BJ's Colourways and Collectibles, 21 Price St, Invercargill, Southland, New Zealand. jans.yarn@clear.net.nz (Random-dyed rayon)
- Quality Yarns, 1 Edward St, Milton, New Zealand. qualityarns@xtra.co.nz. (possum 40%, merino 50%, nylon 10% yarn. Also 110/2 merino yarn in black and white).
- Dea Nominees Ltd, 68 Cambridge St, South Levin, New Zealand. www.deayarns.com.au (space-dyed cotton, rayons, etc)

United Kingdom

- William Hall & Co, 177 Stanley Rd, Cheadle Hulme, Cheadle, Cheshire SK8 6RF, UK. william@hallyarns.fsnet.co.uk (folded viscose rayon, fancy viscose rayon).
- Handweavers Studio, 29 Haroldstone Rd, London, E177 AN, UK. www.handweaversstudio.co.uk (rayon, polyester).

USA

- Halcyon Yarn. www.halcyonyarn.com (10/2 Tencel).

- Webs. 75 Service Center Rd, Northampton, MA, US. www.yarn.com (8/2 Tencel, Susi rayon, bouclé rayon)
- Heritage Spinning & Weaving, 47E Flint St, Lake Orion, MI 48362, US. www.heritagespinning.com. (hand-painted Millington, 45% wool, 55% mohair yarn).
- Textura Trading Company, 116 Pleasant St, #343 Easthampton, MA 01027, US. www.texturatrading.com (T-105 cotton-covered polyester).

# INDEX